THE HOLY TRINITY OF SUCCESSFUL & HEALTHY POLICE ORGANIZATIONS

Improving Leadership, Culture & Wellness

by

CHAD MICHAEL BRUCKNER

ISBN: 979-8-89079-029-3 (Paperback)
ISBN: 979-8-89079-031-6 (Hardback)
ISBN: 979-8-89079-030-9 (Ebook)

This book is dedicated to every police officer. You serve your community, often with little support from within your agency, and are more resilient than you know. I see and hear you. Keep loving everyone and fight cynicism with every breath you have.

Heartfelt gratitude to my wife, Kristen, and children—Lucas, Malia, and Marcus—and pup, Bella. You have provided love, encouragement, support, and loyalty. You've sacrificed time with me to allow me to focus on writing to police officers. I love you to the moon and back!

TABLE OF CONTENTS

INTRODUCTION

Hi, everyone! I'm Chad, and I'm just like you—an ordinary person. First, I wanted to thank you from the bottom of my heart for buying my book. The fact that you're reading this opening section of my book means that you believe enough in my mission to connect and grow together. Or, maybe you're in a bad place at work or at home and you're desperately searching for inspiration like I was. However you ended up here, I'm grateful—truly!

In 2023, mental health professions and clinicians who work with first responders report from the front lines alarming information: more cops are being treated for "organizational betrayal" than trauma and other mental health issues. Why are few discussing this? Because the gatekeepers are also the ones culpable. It makes sense to avoid discussing problems. Few would argue that being exposed to repeated trauma affects first responders in unhealthy ways. What we're learning now, though, is we can recover from trauma in healthy environments. We can heal and live productive lives. I have experienced traumatic events over my lifetime, and it's those experiences that contributed to my resilience.

I have spent the better part of the past four years working to learn the solution that plagues law enforcement. I finally have the answer as to why so many first responders and military personnel are unable to heal and recover: they're serving in environments that are not set up for them to heal. It's like treading water wearing a weighted vest. We can only tread for so long before we succumb. I feel lucky to have made it out alive and intact after twenty-one years of government service, especially considering that many don't. I believe we need a new way to police our communities, and that starts from within.

Method

I will share my *lived experiences* and perspectives in this book. I use *storytelling* as my primary method of influence in this book. Storytelling in advocacy is the practice of using stories about individuals or communities to help build support for a particular policy objective. Storytelling can be a powerful tool for inspiring others to act. It can humanize and contextualize abstract concepts and policy debates and can be used to build a sense of a shared purpose in examining and reforming existing systems of power and oppression. Storytelling helps us build relationships and create community around a particular issue and can be used to motivate disadvantaged populations to speak up and take action. Storytelling can be a valuable tool for seeing, understanding, and responding to injustice and has been used as an effective advocacy tool for centuries. I love telling stories and connecting with people. I never thought I could make a living at it, but here we go.

I commit myself to be honest, direct, considerate, thoughtful, realistic, helpful, and positive. When we pursue societal change, we are guaranteed to stir the pot and ruffle feathers. That can lead to conflict. I understand this and always extend my arms to anyone and everyone. To the antagonists of our life's stories: using our own painful experiences to help the greater body of police officers seems like the only right thing to do. My options were to hide in shame or thrive in sunlight. I made a choice that best serves the policing profession, even at a personal cost. Hiding in shame, which I wanted to do, was counter to my values and mission of always serving people honorably and faithfully. We don't control the actions of others; all we can do is focus on being the best humans we can be and treat everyone according to the Golden Rule. Men can lie or bend the truth to satisfy their positions, but history tends to judge accurately.

Creative Process

I wrote this book by myself and did not have a ghostwriter assist me. I hired an amazing book coach to guide me, only to run out of money to pay him. I was blessed that he introduced me to JETLAUNCH, an independent publisher who is stepping up to get this message out! JETLAUNCH is the reason you're receiving this message arranged in such an impactful format. JETLAUNCH was founded by Chris O'Byrne, a U.S. veteran who understands the importance of service. Chris has a great team of editors who lent their talents to this project. They took my humble message and turned it into a story worth sharing. It truly takes a collaborative effort to bring influential and impactful art to the public. I am by no means labeling this book a best-seller; that's for you to decide. But, if we want to do something impactful for the world, I think it can only be done through collaboration. What you're about to read came from my soul and was molded by many to reach this destination.

I enjoyed the creative process very much. My sixth-grade English teacher Mr. Lagrotte put a black-and-white composition book in my hand, and I have been journaling ever since. I've journaled throughout most of my life, and without knowing it then, my journaling has allowed me to bring this book to you. I've always journaled for myself, yet here I am, writing a book for others.

This process wasn't always easy on my family. I learned in life that to achieve special things requires special effort. I committed four months to this book, which consumed me. I set those expectations with my wife and children. Still, it wasn't easy, as I found myself waking up at 4 a.m. many times to pour out the thoughts swirling in my heart and brain. I truly believed God was working within me to organize all my thoughts and help me write them in a manner that would bring about change.

The commitment I made to this book caused stress in marriage, as time wasn't the only concern. We also struggled to pay our bills for the past year, and those muddy experiences only made this process more authentic to creating something I'm equally proud and nervous about.

My WHY

Speaking openly and authentically is challenging for most of us. This creative process helped me to realize that I engage in passion projects for myself and only share the ones that I think can help others. There hasn't been a calling more significant for me than this book. There were many times I tried to quit, and God tugged on my soul to remind me it's not about me. I even felt him arm me with the courage and strength necessary for the journey. What journey? To change the way police agencies lead and serve. I don't want anyone to experience the shame, guilt, and hopelessness I felt. I know it will continue to happen to people and that's why I almost quit many times. What does it matter? Well, I think showing up for causes that are important matters a great deal. What example am I setting if I don't lead and serve in the same selfless manner you're about to read?

This book was written with one group of people in my mind and heart: police officers. I have such a love for policing and what it can be. I've experienced positive policing and the tangible benefits felt within the community. I've also experienced toxic policing and how it ruins the fabric of "community." This book will not answer all of your questions, and I hope after you read it, you understand how my perspectives can reshape and reimagine American policing in a way that brings back pride and restores nobility. The only way we do that is from the ground up, from within. When we focus on what makes Successful and Healthy Police Organizations, it is clear that agencies can never be healthy and optimal without having well leaders who foster a healthy culture. Our officers are the heartbeat of our departments and demand well leaders guiding, coaching, and mentoring them. Thus, the *Holy Trinity of Leadership, Culture, and Wellness* was born.

Why Now?

American policing is at a crossroads—really, the world if we factor the civil unrest throughout Europe, Asia, and the Middle East. . Policing has become too institutionalized and militarized. In 2019, I sustained a mental and emotional breakdown as the result of unresolved trauma and working in a toxic workplace. Throughout this book, I will share the most intimate parts of my soul as I walk you through my journey. It's all rooted in helping make institutional change so that cops can thrive serving their communities and go home as healthy as possible and take fewer hostages in their personal life.

This book was written from *my lived perspective* as one man living in a broken world. I use my education and knowledge in conjunction with my lived experiences to form an understanding of the world. I love people. I talk to everyone and have friends from all different walks of life. I enjoy meeting new people and learning about them. I'm curious to know one's journey and welcome the opportunity to connect with them even in the lowest of emotional places. We all have varying experiences, so our perspectives will be unique—and that's OK! Somehow along the way in policing, bureaucrats and executives who lead many police departments have forgotten their most people important responsibilities: the community and their officers. It's really that simple. Everything else is fluff and noise, no matter what excuses they offer.

Too many of our citizens resent our profession, and the elephant in the room is that *we* are holding ourselves back from being better. It's true if we look objectively and remove the political and social bias. The cream has not risen to the top in so many departments across America, and it has crushed the profession. Outdated promotional processes, subjective executive selections, political corruption, organizational betrayal, and more. More officers today suffer from poor mental and emotional health from what's going on inside their department than what's going on in the community. Trauma is a real and devastating issue, and I will share plenty of personal stories about trauma. But here's the thing: our brains heal and recover from traumatic incidents. What police officers don't recover from as easily is the politics and corruption inside their own agency. Do you know what kills more police officers than all else combined? Suicide, according to Bluehelp.com. The question that keeps me up at night is: Don't we want to reduce police officer suicide? The reason I struggle to sleep sometimes is because I'm not sure.

Often, plain ole ineptitude that ravages many police departments corrodes the credibility of even the solid officers working at that agency. Whether we admit it or not aloud, police officers can be highly judgmental. We can judge someone for a rumor we heard thirdhand and tell ourselves we absolutely believe it. Paranoia, cynicism, and jaded hearts have suffocated many police departments, and many officers identify themselves with the title "officer" because, generationally, we passed down bad habits. If we're trying to build relationships, why are we leading with our title—which by the way, isn't the most endearing title? It's not supposed to be, and that's the point. American policing must adapt—and fast. We can do it, and I hope this book serves as some form of inspiration.

American policing has long sacrificed our collective self-care and now has countless unhealthy, dysfunctional, or even toxic workplace cultures. Most inside the profession acknowledge the problems, yet we struggle to identify the right thought leaders to lead the reimagining revolution that American policing requires right now. I'll take it even further in this book. If we analyze corruption and dysfunction in all organizations and government bodies, I lay out the stance that it's largely because of unresolved **childhood trauma**. Supervisors in all professions (and even in the federal government) **take hostages** if they don't heal from their own pain first.

This book will ruffle feathers for some currently enjoying a comfortable lifestyle at the expense of their communities and officers. For most cops and leaders, I pray and hope this is refreshing and the dose of inspiration you need right now. I left policing in 2021 disappointed and cynical about what I saw inside my agency and other agencies around me. I continued to ask myself, "I can't be the only one who recognizes how messed up this is, right?" Our citizens are not the enemy. I fought real enemies, and Americans are not them.

Tens of thousands of American police officers are afraid to speak their truths for fear of retribution. Think about that. Only in unhealthy cultures created by toxic leaders can employees not speak the truth. If organizations are healthy, there isn't a culture of fear and distrust. Countless police agencies operate unhealthy cultures and are "taking hostages" along the way. Get used to me saying that term; I will reference it a lot anytime there is interpersonal conflict in the workplace and certain colleagues think it's OK to take others hostage with their emotions and tactics.

American democracy, which seems to be under scrutiny, requires loyal and noble patriots to protect us. We need community members who choose to be selfless. They raise their hands to serve. To serve others. According to their needs and laws. For the people. These noble police officers raise their hands and choose to serve. In return, society rewards them and celebrates them for their sacrifice. Loyalty isn't blind—it's earned.

I don't believe the majority of Americans hate police officers. In fact, I think the majority love and support the police. I imagine they want, as I do, healthy and trained police officers patrolling their communities. What's happening right now to the average police officer in America is a shame. Our media has depicted them as the sole bad guys. This politically motivated rhetoric divides communities. A recent conversation I had with a teacher friend reminded me of the importance of **fairness**. He told me that the first step to take when attempting to maintain order in a group is to deploy fairness. Simply being equitable in the beginning helps create a culture of trust. A leader can't rely on that for long as the group is constantly looking for additional leadership. But he told me that it's imperative to be fair and equitable in the classroom and that without fair treatment, there would be no classroom management. The criminal justice system as a whole is grossly unfair, and we must come together to grow and heal as a community.

Our noble profession has been highjacked by political officials who largely don't understand policing and are taking their guidance from the inept autocrats they select to lead their police departments. The **ineffective** police executive, at best, resigns or retires on their own accord. We have been selecting leaders based on improper metrics, and there lies the problem. It's a generational self-perpetuating cycle. The American policing profession is on life support, and we need thought leaders to come together if we're going to save it. Together, we will have to talk about the ugly parts of the profession that few discuss publicly. This helps us come out of the shadows and begin the work of change.

I have committed myself to studying **leadership** for the past twenty-three years. I still have so much to learn. Everything in this book is something I experienced or have firsthand knowledge of. It took me many years to realize how much experience I have and the positive effects it can have on the lives of others. You will read many of my personal lived experiences to help you understand **mental and emotional health**. These are my experiences, and I share them with you as a source of inspiration in times you may need it.

One thing I felt at my lowest was **isolation**. I really believed that no one in the world could relate to what I was going through. It was that hopelessness that no one would be able to help me that caused me to contemplate ending my life. The reality is, rarely do any of us face challenges that haven't been faced already by others right within our communities. That's why connection is so critical for us as social creatures. We develop **resilience** and **gratitude** largely by being connected to people or missions important to us. By being vulnerable and connecting with one another, we are provided with opportunities to help each other through our own lived experiences. This is the essence of what America is: a blended community in which we stand together for one another.

Today, I document this journey of my mental health experiences to serve you in whatever way I can help you. I'm not a licensed professional. I always share my intimate reflections with the understanding that these experiences are near to my heart. I share them with the utmost trust that they'll be used for good. We're a community, and if we don't come together now, I worry for future generations of Americans who will need healthy, trained, and service-minded police officers in our communities.

The world is messy and more so than ever. Society loves to paint us into black-and-white boxes when in reality, the world is gray and chaotic. This book was written for two distinct purposes: 1) to help provide a framework to make culture change in American policing and 2) to help those same stakeholders develop the courage and resilience needed to make that hard change.

In addition to providing police organizations with the courage and information to make a culture change, I also shared methods and experiences I used to navigate highly dysfunctional and stressful times and come out the other side thriving. I'm not special in any way. I'm you, an **everyday person**. It's only by being beaten down many times that I found ways to develop higher levels of resilience. Who couldn't use that right now? Enjoy the reading, and don't forget to share with me your tips and tricks for weathering storms.

Most of the challenging pursuits in life require little more than grit, curiosity, and courage to endure. The policing profession has become a wasteland for proper talent because of political subterfuge, inept leadership, and toxic cultures. My only hope from this book is that it generates real and honest discussions about how police can improve from within. It's the only way.

As a police life coach, I ask a lot of "what" questions, such as, "What does your morning look like when you don't wake up and give yourself enough time?" By asking these "what" questions, clients are able to coach themselves through self-guided reflection. They build their confidence by answering questions about their life. It's an empowering process! I will attempt to do the same thing in this book—to build your confidence and show you that you're more capable than you realize by asking many "what" questions. These questions may be rhetorical, but really they are designed solely for you to answer them in your head. This process will help you make the change by creating neurological pathways. Speak it into existence!

To every cop and executive who's grieved the loss of a career they loved, there is a better way. Cops aren't bad people; we're just policing wrong. Let's meet in the middle and have hard conversations to discuss real solutions.

PROLOGUE

The Voice Wears a Mask

November 29,2019
6:28 a.m.

My brain was racing. *The Voice* wouldn't stop talking to me. "You're embarrassing your family," he told me. "You're going to hold them back." *The Voice* kept saying it, and I didn't know how to make it stop. As I walked out of the building, I continued to argue with *The Voice*. There wasn't anyone around, however; *The Voice* was in my head.

I was tired. Really tired. I had just finished a twelve-hour night shift and was heading home. I was depressed. I wanted a beer. Or a drug. I thought about them both. Something to help me not feel the shame and guilt I was carrying around. The mere thoughts of shame added more shame. It was all so heavy, and I couldn't imagine a scenario where I'd be able to get the giant rock off me.

The Rock of Shame.

It was the early morning after Thanksgiving. I finished my shift at 6 a.m. The highway was quiet and long. I didn't see another car on the road. It was over thirty-five miles of travel, mostly highway miles home. Everyone was home with their families except for me, and self-loathing ruled my headspace. The depression was growing by the day; I couldn't find a way to quiet *The Voice* in my head. He was saying horrible things to me.

About me.

"YOU lost."

"YOU failed."

Then, he got personal with me!

"Everybody finally figured YOU out."

"YOU'RE a fraud."

Wow, what a nasty person that *Voice* is.

But then it started getting scary as the days went by.

"There's nowhere to hide now, bro. They know all about YOU."

"YOU might as well kill yourself because it's over."

Looking back, I wish I could wrap my arms around that guy and tell him he's going to be OK. I sit here today writing this book with a clear understanding of how emotions work. They're fleeting, and no matter our emotions, they will end eventually. Is there someone you wish you could wrap your arms around today and remind them it's going to be OK?

Our brains are the most complex organ in our bodies, and mine was in pain. What I didn't know then was that I was injured. Not physically but morally, mentally, and emotionally. I am diagnosed with post-traumatic stress disorder (PTSD) related to my combat experience. I remember the first time feeling anxious when I came back. There was road construction and I panicked and ran over several cones. My brain tricked me into thinking there was a roadside bomb hidden in those cones. That's what PTSD looked like for me seven months after not experiencing combat any longer. I remember how sweaty my hands and shirt were. I was 25 and had no idea about mental and emotional health. After being diagnosed by the VA, I didn't address this medically for several years. Instead, I self-medicated with alcohol and, on occasion, drugs. I was very private because of the dislike I was feeling for myself. The shame built by the day in my late twenties.

"What is wrong with YOU?" *The Voice* yelled at me.

"Are you a drug addict?" the real Chad asked *The Voice.*

My life has been so amazing, with wonderful blessings. It's because of those that I refused to acknowledge the growing problem that would soon force me at a crossroads. I needed professional help because I couldn't manage my life on my own.

That was very hard for me to admit in the beginning. I tried to control as much as possible in my life. I just came home from leading combat missions and found myself as a police officer.

"YOU could lose YOUR job," *The Voice* liked to remind me if I asked for help.

My second child was born the same month I was promoted to detective. My wife was a teacher and stayed home with our second for an extended period without pay. I remember driving home from the hospital with our second in the backseat. The reality hit me hard. I looked in my rearview mirror and saw my 2 ½-year old in one seat and my newborn in the other. I looked at my beautiful wife in the passenger seat and felt an overwhelming sense of worry and anxiety. My stomach had knots, I had sweaty hands, I couldn't catch my breath for a second, and my surroundings were briefly distorted. I pulled the car over and gathered myself. It's funny because my wife, Kristen, and I talked about that incident recently, and neither of us was experienced enough to recognize that as a warning sign. It was 2012, six years after mistaking cones for a roadside bomb, and I had my second panic attack, yet I didn't recognize it then.

I felt the pressure to be a great husband and father. I want to be the best dad possible. I loved being a police officer and wanted to be the best detective. It was possible, too. To be the best, it required real good, decent, hard police work. When I'm passionately involved in my work, it can consume me. I always worked with a chip on my shoulder. I wanted to be the best at everything.

Life was and is good. It's also messy, and those conflicting perspectives used to add to my shame. Kristen and I were building so many memories together, and my family was my guiding beacon. The trauma and subsequent shame manifestations were a separate part of me. A part I wanted to hide from everyone, even me. Shame began to develop in my subconscious. I'm sure I made decisions based largely on my shame. Do you think you're carrying shame to the point that it affects your decision-making?

By the time my third child was born in 2017, the stress was overwhelming. I was not a helpful husband. I stopped doing things around the house that I was used to doing. I was drinking every day, which became hard drinking most days. I had beer stocked in both fridges and was at the liquor store weekly, picking up an assortment of liquors. Nights were the worst for me. The fear and anxiety in the evenings was unbearable sometimes.

The worst was yet to come.

By the time my youngest turned 1, my war-related nightmares from a decade and a half earlier returned. Looking back, the stress had boiled over, and I was also having police-related nightmares, which were new. They picked up with frequency and were more intense and graphic than anything I'd experienced in the past. I couldn't believe this was something new to deal with. The signs of my decline were there; no one around me—including myself as a trained mental health peer support officer—recognized them. Life moves very fast, and if we're not careful, we miss the clear warning signs in a friend's troubled life.

I was 38 years old and desperate for a change. Truthfully desperate for help. I had seen a therapist once several years earlier and stopped. I missed out on a promotional opportunity at work. I was really hoping for it and believed it was time. I was an accomplished detective and was on the verge of attaining a master's degree. I led my agency in proactive arrests during my tenure there and was also active in the community. I demonstrated a high degree of leadership skills throughout my tenure and had over fifteen years of practical and dynamic leadership experience to support my promotion.

My declining mental and emotional health was exacerbated by an unethical and biased police chief who was hired in 2018. I had more leadership experience than the chief of police, and I found myself caught up in a situation where the chief began targeting me. As a result, a new demon entered my life that would end up being a fight I couldn't handle. This new demon was the Self-Worth Monster of Shame.

We're going to get into all of it throughout this book. Self-doubt was always there. Hiding and waiting. Success lied to me, and it was time to learn the truth. The Demon of Trauma found a friend and together they attacked my self-worth until I almost gave up. What I've learned about myself is that when I feel fear,

I usually choose to flee. Unless there's no other option, and I take up arms. First choice, run. Last choice, fight. The more I learned about the unethical and immoral behaviors occurring at the hands of the leaders I was supposed to trust, I realized that the only way to preserve my mental and emotional health—and my family—was to leave the organization and chart a new course.

It would be the hardest thing I've done. I was angry and sad. I was depressed and using substances to cope. I was not mentally or emotionally in a good place, and the thoughts of harming myself increased. I would gain clarity later to realize an ugly truth: I worked in a profession with many other broken souls, and those people were taking hostages. The official end of my youth occurred when my mentor betrayed me, and that's the inspiration for writing this book. You, too, may be working in a toxic culture, and by sharing our scars with one another, we can help to repair the countless broken cultures in American policing.

I focus on the blessings around me. Gratitude has tremendous benefits in our lives and helps us chart a path toward higher levels of resilience. I knew the only way to save myself, recover, and live a life of significance was to LOVE. So, that's what I've done for the past four years. Loving relentlessly and learning what FREEDOM really means.

My hope is you read this book and make whatever changes you need to make in your personal life and career. If you're an executive, I pray every day that God gives you the courage to lead with distinction and grace.

ACT I

FALL

CHAPTER 1

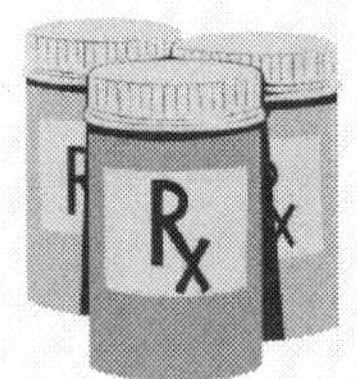

SHAME

"CHANGE IS INEVITABLE; GROWTH IS OPTIONAL."
~ JOHN MAXWELL

6.18.19

When I drove into work that day, I had a sense of pride that I used to feel a lot more of. The night before, my longtime partner Nick Oropeza and I dropped off a suspect at the county jail that we arrested for a shooting. These cases admittedly had been fewer for me. Maybe crime was lower. Maybe my energy to dig up the extra cases was less. Maybe a bit of both.

I was seated at my desk when I was notified to meet with administration. It caught me off guard, and I assumed they wanted to congratulate me on the shooting arrests. After all, we spent several months investigating, and we achieved a good outcome. I figured I would hear, "Congrats Bruck." I walked into the chief's office, and he was seated along with the lieutenant. Something was wrong.

My meeting was brief. To the point. Less than five minutes. It culminated with me being reassigned back to patrol. I remember being so shell-shocked that a single tear rolled down my cheek. I left the office and walked down a long hall. My very first thought was, *How am I going to explain this?* I felt panic start to wash over me.

What you need to understand about me, and maybe you're the same way, is I was too trusting. I assumed everyone came into the workforce wanting to make a positive impact and be a team player. I was about to get a cruel lesson on politics and workplace culture.

I walked out the chief's door and down the long hallway out to the police cars. I was still shocked about what happened and hadn't processed it yet. That's the thing about life. For some of us, it takes a while to process events and evaluate emotional outcomes. I left the police department and called Kristen. She's a teacher and off during the summer. When I told her what happened, she immediately quipped, "Well, I guess you're leaving there." I remember those words offending me. "No!" I shouted into the phone. "I'll get through this. I chose to stay here. Maybe this is a good thing."

I was a fixer and a positive thinker. That can be a force for good or a leash from true potential. See, I would often interject myself into friends' situations and try to help—*over* help. Try to fix their problems and help them because I love them. If we direct our energy to things we have control over, we enhance our chances of reaching our full potential.

I decided to grit my teeth and not show that I was affected. I was strong enough to handle this. I was the ace detective being demoted for what everyone knew was personal reasons. But! I'm going to take the high road! I'm going to be positive!

Day by day, the emotionally depleted me began to fester on the demotion. The shame started to sink in. *I'm going back to the same job I had seven years ago when I was a rookie. What will people think?*

Day by day, it got worse. I was already on empty.

What will my kids think?
Is my wife ashamed of me?
Is it me?
Wait, it's me, isn't it?
Oh God, it's me.

The shame deepened. I became depressed. Alcohol became my only lifeline to feeling somewhat normal. But I hated myself. I couldn't look myself in the mirror without the voice in my head reminding me that I was a scumbag and everyone finally knew it. I started avoiding mirrors at home. But now I was a patrolman and had to put on a brave face. On top of that, I was working with three guys that I knew for a long time, and somehow that brought me more anxiety than working with cops I wasn't as close with. They were so welcoming and gracious when I came back. I felt their empathy, and that was a HUGE deal for me at that time. Lord knows I needed it for the battle that lay ahead.

This was me being positive, believing that being reassigned to patrol was a good thing for me and that my agency was doing the right thing for the community. Over the next couple of months, the reality hit as my shame grew.

What if this was punitive? I began questioning.

Looking back, I should have been more aware to recognize the potential for corruption at my agency since the hiring of the new Chief, Matthew Pathe. I was aware of him working against the old chief behind the scenes. I was aware of the self-serving behavior. I was aware of the immoral acts. I overlooked them because I'm too trusting. After I didn't get promoted, every officer who did not get promoted had concerns about the improprieties of the promotional exam. Chief Pathe came up in the department. He was my first-line supervisor with detectives, and we spent a lot of time off duty together. He was a mentor to me. For years leading up to his appointment to chief, he was critical of the testing company, which was run as a side gig by a neighboring chief.

When Chief Pathe was up for the position, our municipality hired the testing company he did not favor. The company belonged to another active-duty chief who bordered our town. After an exhaustive process with applicants from different states, Chief Pathe came out number one and was selected. It shouldn't surprise anyone that the chief came out number one because he had developed a personal relationship with the founders of the testing company. Twelve months later, the chief selected the same testing company to promote four sergeants. It's interesting to watch leaders make decisions that you know go against their personal values. Chief Pathe didn't favor the testing company, but after they selected him as the number one candidate for chief, did he feel obligated to retain them even though he didn't think they turned out a good product? Did Chief Pathe getting promoted feel a need to scratch the back of the other chief at the expense of building the best teams possible? These are interesting questions to consider as we move through this book.

Upon examining the sergeants who were promoted, none of them had military experience, which is important in terms of leadership ethics and experience. One of the candidates was only a police officer for two years. Every single position of influence in the department was carefully crafted by the chief to not have one dissenting opinion. Not one.

From the lieutenant to the detective sergeant, he has installed "yes people" who would not sniff out his sneaky behaviors. More importantly, none of the leaders he installed were a threat to him. Some of them were underperformers he chose to insulate his command. He even cut off ties with the town manager in an attempt to further silo himself. That's the playbook of sneaky people. Transparency is the enemy.

The Morning after Thanksgiving

The hopelessness was too much. Shame was winning. I had been self-medicating for months and was engaged in harmful behavior. I was so private with my pain. Leading up to today, I had passing thoughts of completing suicide. I didn't want to do it, and I was thinking it through to see what that would look like for my family. I kept thinking of how much shame they would feel if I took my life. I was also thinking of my own shame. It was overwhelming. This day felt different.

I was so sad driving home from work. I felt defeated and ready to give up. That's not my normal disposition. The pain was causing me to look for ways to stop or pause it. There were no other cars on the turnpike. It was a holiday, after all. There are several bridges along the turnpike, and as I came upon the first one, I was ruminating on my situation and imagined driving my car off the bridge. I pictured a fiery crash and no more pain. That mental image brought me comfort in the moment. I continued to drive on. As I approached the second bridge, I imagined the same thing and felt more peace and optimism. This happened again, and it made me cry. I had so much going on in my life and felt powerless over all of it.

However, that was a distortion, and looking back, my tears were a realization that I could do this. I could get help and not leave my family. I could overcome my personal shame and be better. I knew this logically, but it was still extremely challenging to remain objective in the moment. I was literally trying to win a battle with my brain, and I think that day, I decided to start fighting back.

I remember the first time I told Kristen I was thinking of ending my life. I told her I wasn't going to do it, and I was starting to figure my way out of the darkness. It was hard as I saw the fear on her face. Her fear added more shame. What was I doing to my family?

I had already been in therapy for a couple months, and the shame of not progressing more than I thought I should was another shame pancake on top of my mountain of pancakes. Kristen and I decided that I have to share everything on my journey. We must connect on it all if we want to survive. We take our marriage and family duties seriously, and she was absolutely right. I needed to lean on her, and that was tough. But she made it special for me. There was not one instance during my recovery where Kristen made me feel guilty for what I was going through. I saw so much growth in her as she remained loyal and supportive of me.

Don't Judge Us When We're Down

Have you ever consciously pondered what holds you back from doing the things you really want? It could be a lack of resources. Perhaps it's poor support or confidence. The more I thought about life and failure, I realized that my shame has been a major disruptor for me.

In the life of a police officer, shame can manifest for us in a variety of ways. For example, police officers may experience shame due to the public scrutiny they may face if they make mistakes or misjudgments in their line of duty. Officers may feel ashamed for something they felt they had no control over, such as an incident in which they were forced to use force.

Additionally, police officers may feel shame when they are accused of misconduct or when members of their own department criticize their performance. Officers may also struggle with the guilt of not being able to intervene in a crime that resulted in a victim's harm or death. Finally, police officers may feel ashamed when they witness their peers engaging in certain inappropriate or unethical behaviors. Unfortunately, police culture today can be toxic and much shame results from what goes on behind the doors of our police departments.

After being demoted in 2019, I felt tremendous shame as a result. A couple of years ago, I began examining shame in my life. Where did it come from? Why did I carry it? What can I do to rid myself of it? The more I self-discovered, the more confusing it was. I found parts of myself that I absolutely loved; I also saw parts that I hated and wanted to change. The deeper I went, I found layers to myself that needed adjustment. It's all rather fascinating to me how complex the human brain is. The more I dug, the scarier it got. When I evaluated my past regrettable behavior and thoughts, one thing jumped out to me: I carried around a lot of shame and it placed many obstacles in my life.

Over the past several years, I committed myself to recovering from shame and charted a new way forward. A better way. My hope is you read this work and find human connection within your own shame. When we share our shame and embrace optimism, we can develop into humble and learned servants of God. Imagine a life where we develop the consistent momentum needed to be more confident and successful. That's what I wanted and chose to pursue. First, I had to walk through the ugly parts of me in order to identify my deficiencies and make change.

Shame takes hold in my life when I recognize my regretful behavior. When I made mistakes as a youngster or experienced failures, instead of embracing and learning from them, I built up a cache of shame. I wasted opportunities to develop a higher level of resilience. The weight wore me down over the years.

I have chosen to pursue a professional path that will be very difficult. Changing how a profession leads and thinks is never easy. There will be many challenges in my way, and I will have to find a way through them. It's been the hardest thing I've ever done. War wasn't close. I had to first reconcile the broken parts of my soul. I cannot go into a hard mission without being as centered as possible. I practice vulnerability as much as possible because I have experienced just how powerful human connection is. Human connection helps us build resilience and have the allies necessary to fight demons. Through every setback in life, I didn't recognize the opportunity to embrace my pain so that I could build resilience. Instead, I choose comfort and safety. I thought to myself, *What if I run into my trauma instead of away from it?* That's what I decided to do—chase my shame.

I decided to put shame on the run so she couldn't hurt me anymore. The more shame I encountered in dark hallways, the less afraid I felt. Shame is ugly and scary, but I learned she can't kill us. Heck, shame doesn't even bite. I've fallen many times in my life, and in 2019 I fell hard. The shame I felt was so severe that I thought of ending my life. Instead of suicide, I chose to fight back. It was the fight of my life, for my life.

By the time my policing career was concluding in 2021, I had learned how to wear a mask to survive. The organizational culture was so toxic that I had no choice but to run away to survive. It was the only perceived option available to me to preserve my life, family, and morality. Instinctively, in high-stress environments, my brain seeks solitude. I will leave wherever I am to seek refuge. If I'm somewhere already physically safe, I will hunker down. At my police department, I felt safer on the streets within our community than I did inside our own building. The brotherhood/sisterhood died there years ago. My mental health suffered so severely that I spent months ruminating about ending my life. The shame was strong, and I needed help fast.

As I began to tackle shame, I had to first unpack my life. I identified many sectors of my soul that required emergency surgery. Like a surgeon would do, I committed myself to heal in a disciplined and educated manner. But unlike a surgeon, this was more art for me than science. I approach recovery from a platform of growth and philosophy. The better I learned to control my brain—and not let it drive me—the better I was at winning in life. What an epiphany!

I abruptly retired from law enforcement after thirteen years and bought an existing private investigations firm. Truthfully, I did not run toward entrepreneurship. I ran away from policing, from the toxicity there. And most of all, I ran from my shame. The hard truth is many times, we leave jobs within the same profession because of the people and not the job itself. Put me in this category.

I've experienced professional success. I was promoted to sergeant at 20 and am a former Non-Commissioned Officer of the Year for my brigade. At 24, I was promoted to staff sergeant and led a nine-man infantry squad in Iraq. Leadership has been in my DNA for as long as I can remember. In war, we captured four of the top ten high-value targets in our sector. All my soldiers were promoted, and four out of the nine were promoted to sergeant. One of them is still in and serving as an infantry platoon sergeant. The other is a master sergeant in Special Operations. I have always invested in my men and molded them as much as possible. It's not about me; it's about them and their development.

The main question on my mind lately is reflecting on how we got to a place where so many leaders put themselves before the mission and their teammates.

I returned home from war at 25 and had my sights set on policing. I rose through the ranks quickly and was promoted to detective in four years. Over the next several years, I was part of an undercover unit that made over 200 felony arrests. We tangibly could feel the difference in the community. Drug dealers stopped coming into our town because of our reputation. It was an incredible experience, and to this day, I have never felt more pride or a sense of community than I did during those three years.

By 2018 we hired a new chief, and the culture began to change almost immediately. I recognized it then and had a conversation with our leadership team. I understand how leadership and organizational culture mesh together, and I was trying to be helpful.

Our chief had his hand in promoting every leader in the department, and he created a culture of "yes" people. I know every leader currently serving at my former agency. While they are uniquely talented in their own rights, not one of them will push back on the chief. This was done by design to curate a culture of fear, selfishness, and blind ambition. The more I talked with police officers in other agencies, the more I realized how common this is. I will examine how we got here and what we can do to fight our way out of it.

I've been part of eleven organizational cultures: good, bad, and apathetic. When executives begin the regiment of secrecy and backdoor channels, I have experienced how it plays out. It rarely ends up in a good place. This is why oversight is critical. Leaders are human and require supervision. Without proper supervision, humans, regardless of rank or status, are left to their devices. If leaders are not morally minded, we fall to our baseline. Leadership is a way of life for me. All my actions are decided through a lens of how my actions affect the world around me. I wake up each day aiming to model good behavior for others. I fail most days and continue to work to be the best version of myself.

"I'm going to die if I don't leave here," I repeated to myself many times over the final eighteen months in policing.

So with an infantryman's version of a solid plan, I took early retirement to chase whatever dreams I could find in the business world. I had so much shame that it was difficult for me to think about my policing career. I went through all the emotions—anger, resentment, sadness, SHAME. I couldn't figure out why I was feeling ashamed. I was trying to be part of solutions and serve our community. Why did this happen to me? I imagine these are typical feelings and thoughts for anyone during a major life transition. Here's what I knew for sure: I refused to leave my family behind without me. Therefore, believing I would die if I stayed, I had no choice but to leave.

Having no marketable skills, I had to find my way in the world. I believed my experience in public service wouldn't translate well to entrepreneurship, so I added even more shame to my already full plate. I went from being a sought-after detective to being 40 years old cold messaging people on LinkedIn who I thought could help me.

SHAME!

"Hello, I'm a new business owner and don't have any experience in entrepreneurship. Would you please have ten to fifteen minutes to jump on a call so I can ask you questions?"

These messages went out like hotcakes. I had to fight through my personal shame. Real or not, it's what was raging within me.

"What if people ask why I left policing?" is a question I had to force myself to embrace and deal with.

"I spoke out against corruption and was punished for it," is what I wanted to say.

"It was time for a change, and I'm exited to be a PI now running a business," is what I actually said.

Entrepreneurship is hard. I knew that a strong network is powerful, and I was a guppie in the ocean of commerce. I had a couple of buddies in business who were tremendously helpful. The rest was up to me. The business world did not feel sorry for me. I was desperate and fearful, which were not good combinations. I was also fiercely determined to prove my critics wrong.

It was the first time in my life that I had people publicly doubt me. Leaders who were supposed to mentor and encourage were anything but. I knew I needed support, and going at it alone wasn't going to help me reach our company goals.

In 2021 I attended a veteran entrepreneurs conference. This nonprofit organization was investing in me, and it felt good to be chosen and poured into. It was just what I needed to help overcome my shame. As a new entrepreneur, I was flooded with many emotions. I felt tremendous freedom and safety in my new role. It was on me, and no one could walk into my office anymore and hurt me. That was when I first learned of Maslow's Hierarchy of Needs. By just not being in that selfish environment anymore, I felt safe. It was empowering. I talked to another cop who left my agency at the same time, and we shared in each other's safety. I felt like I made it home from war again. It shouldn't be that way in our workplace cultures.

The fear I had in early entrepreneurship was significant. I have a pension coming to me that I can't touch for another nine years, and I must lead my family's efforts to provide. It was a new and uncomfortably dangerous feeling. It still is some days. Entrepreneurship is not for the faint of heart. Big swings in earnings, periods of no cash, competitors, economic factors, etc. I can't tell you how many times I asked, "Did I make a selfish decision by not staying in law enforcement?"

More shame.

It's wise and prudent to consider all sides.

The answer has been and will always be no. I was unsafe there. I was being targeted for speaking out against the corruption. I had no choice but to leave.

It was a selfless decision to leave, actually.

I put my family before myself or the community.

God knows I loved serving the community and was good at it. It's not hard for me to collaborate due to my selfless heart. I had such a knack for arresting violent offenders one minute and then helping an elderly lady carry in her groceries the next. I loved it all and was darn good at it. When 2022 arrived, it was the first time in my life that I decided to address the shame I was carrying. Truthfully, I was suffering. Shame was winning, and if I wasn't careful, I was going to lose the battle. I decided that the only way I could personally win was by exposing my own shame.

Shame of my policing career ending before I hoped.
Shame of the bad things I did/saw in war.
Shame for the treatment of how cops treated each other.
Shame for drinking alcohol and using drugs to self-medicate my pain.
Shame of feeling mentally and emotionally weak.
Shame of what my colleagues continue to say as rumors get back to me.
Shame of being abandoned by my agency.
Shame of my agency targeting me.
Shame of working for a narcissist and not doing more to help the cops still there.
Shame of how I treated my wife.
Shame of how I resented God.
Shame of the lies I've told when I was afraid.
Shame of missing friends' funerals.
Shame of having suicidal ideation.
Shame of thinking of driving my car off a bridge.
Shame of not having money.

I had to finally face my personal shame to become the man I wanted to be. We don't become genuine, authentic, and deep souls without walking through our internal fires first. I had to address it all. Here's the most profound discovery I made...

All the behaviors and things that happened to me are in the PAST. I spent so much time and energy worrying about things that are long over. I was able to develop a plan and routine to attack my shame. It was really hard—lots of messy moments. These messy moments still happen, and that's OK! Here's the second most profound thing I discovered: we all have shame.

Think of your shame and how much it's weighed you down. Imagine your life without it. I still carry shame, but only a fraction of what I once did. Shame is a master restrictor, and if we don't break ties with her, we'll be bound forever. Shame has been the single largest handcuff in my life, and I'm learning how to shed the shackles. It's been freeing; I encourage you to try.

Shame has a twin sister, Guilt, and she can be a handful too. We don't have to carry Shame and Guilt. We can work to shed and free ourselves of their binds. I have a feeling you'll be able to generate momentum and be better prepared to go after your dreams and passions that bring you joy. Maybe life handed you a shit sandwich. That sucks, and I'll share the sandwich with you if you want. At some point, though, we will eat the whole sandwich and then decide where to go next. Resilience is emboldened by our shame. Here are the top five things I did that you can too to reduce the shame you're carrying:

1. **Acknowledge and accept your feelings.** Allow yourself to feel whatever emotions come up when you experience shame, and don't try to push them away. Sitting with your feelings can help you gain understanding and start to peel away the layers of shame. This also helps to build our resilience. The more we face our shame, the better we'll recover from it. This was the hardest part for me and the most rewarding in terms of progress. It's OK not to be OK, but it's not OK to stay not OK.

2. **Have a support system.** Find a friend you can reach out to and open up to—someone who won't judge or shame you for your feelings. Talking to a trusted friend can help

you work through the emotions around your shame and provide an outlet for safely expressing yourself. I have a strong inner circle that I trust with the most vulnerable parts of my life. Human connection is required when we desire to shed our guilt and shame.

3. **Be a master at self-compassion.** Many of us can be incredibly cruel to ourselves with the judgments that arise when we experience shame. It's important to be kind to yourself and practice self-compassion in order to let go of the shame and move forward. The more negative thoughts we have about ourselves, the easier it is to believe those thoughts. We are human beings and, therefore, must always remember that failures are opportunities to learn and *improve*.
4. **Seek professional help.** If you find yourself struggling with deep-seated shame, it could be a sign that you need to seek help from a professional therapist. A therapist can help you uncover the root of your feelings and provide tools to help you process and move past the shame. At one time, I had four therapists who all provided different therapies that worked independently of each other to attack my PTSD, fear, shame, and self-esteem. Our brains are the most complex organ in our bodies, and thousands of police officers in the Unites States are starving their brains of knowledge and robbing their brains of the ability to recover.
5. **Sharing is caring.** When we are vulnerable to our struggles, it fosters deeper connections to others and helps us find allies in our battles. Moreover, sharing our shame helps us to develop resilience and humility. The hardest thing for me on my journey was sharing my flaws and struggles. I felt that I deserved them, and it was difficult to admit. Once I did, though, there was much weight taken off my shoulders.

My pain is different than yours. Yours is different than mine. But we all know when something hurts. Let's share that more with each other. In our pain are opportunities to connect, learn, and grow together. I hope that my being vulnerable and sharing private experiences in my life provides you with the courage to tackle your own demons. We can lead together and make the world around us safer and more collaborative.

As you finish this chapter, I imagine you're like me. Reflecting on your own journey. Do you have some painful memories that come up in which you were on the wrong side of things? Is there shame you avoided for so long that it held you back? Here's a call to action for you.

Reach out to someone that you hurt. Explain to them what was going on inside of you when you did that behavior. Apologize and ask for collaboration. Humility will repair your relationship, and ego will divide it.

So, here's your call to action!
Shed the shame.
Garbage the guilt.
Don't get pushed around.
Own your behavior.
The shame is worse in your head.
Heal your baggage.
Believe in your badass self.

CHAPTER II

ROOTS

"I'VE LEARNED THAT PEOPLE WILL FORGET WHAT YOU DID, BUT PEOPLE WILL NEVER FORGET HOW YOU MADE THEM FEEL."
~ MAYA ANGELOU

I want you to know a little about me and where I came from to help you understand it's our unique experiences that contribute to our decision-making and values. Where we come from and what we experience have direct correlations to how we serve as police officers.

I was born in 1980 in Philadelphia. My dad, Mike, was raised in an abusive and dysfunctional home in Philadelphia. At 17, he left his house to join the U.S. Air Force. My mom, Robin, is from Norristown, Pennsylvania, and the oldest of five. My parents met at the local community college and were engaged six months later. My mom was 19 when they got married; my dad was 23. I was born soon after my mom turned 22; I was their first child, followed by my sister, Lindsay, and brother, Alex, whom we call A.J.

Would you believe me if I told you Lindsay is a registered nurse and married a police officer? How about that AJ is a police officer in the same county where we grew up? Remember I was telling you how our experiences shape us? Well, our childhood experiences compelled us all to go into professions focused on serving others. How have your childhood experiences affected your life and career? We will discuss this more later, so don't worry if you're just getting comfortable.

I grew up in a loving and affectionate family. I had a great childhood. We made tons of heartwarming memories, and my parents poured into us with love, compassion, and an intense desire to be good humans. We also had challenges, like many families, and had to find ways to overcome them. As long as I can remember, I've learned to successfully co-mingle the positive and negative always present in my life. Don't we all have good and bad things in our lives? I know we can focus on the good in our lives without ignoring the negative elements. That's resilience in essence.

Bankruptcy

In 1991, we suffered a financial hardship that upended our life. My father owned a construction company and there was a housing bubble in the late '80s that caused him to go bankrupt. My parents had to sell the dream home that my dad just built three years earlier. We moved to an older house in our same town. It was eerily right around when *Rocky V* was released, and in that movie, Rocky's family experienced financial hardship and had to sell everything. They moved back into a rowhome in South Philadelphia. From a big house to a smaller one on the other side of town, we were going through the same thing in our family. My mom recalls that time as miserable for her.

We moved in the summer of 1991, the summer I was going into middle school. I was nervous about middle school, and the bankruptcy added another layer to my life. It was at that time I started biting my nails. It was the first time in my life I adopted a coping strategy to deal with my stress. I was 10 years old and one of the youngest in my class.

Money problems persisted throughout the '90s and worsened as I entered high school. This was when times were the leanest. Money was so tight that I didn't eat lunch at school during my senior year. My grades suffered. I ended up quitting the baseball team with just a couple games left out of shame of not being as good as my peers. I was carrying baggage before I ever took a trip.

We were a proud family; many were back then. You didn't know what was going on behind your neighbor's door. During this time, my parents were doing all they could to be present and engaged while also figuring out how to pay the electric and milkman (yes, we had a milkman!). There were occasions when the utility worker came over to shut off the electric and my dad and he were arguing in the front yard. From bounced checks to avoiding the incoming phone calls, it was just normal for us. We didn't really know any different. We recognized the problems; my family does a fairly good job at communicating. It came down to a simple feeling of safety: we knew we were loved by our parents. In our family, we don't have to be perfect to give and receive love. Were you loved as a child? Did you have negative experiences as a child? What did you do to overcome? What can you do today to keep going?

My Dad – Mike Bruckner

My dad is my hero, mostly due to his imperfections, vulnerability, and resiliency. I watched this man time and time again get up after every fall. He was in therapy for years, and as a kid, I saw him committing himself to be the best family man he could be. My dad was still working through his childhood trauma; there were unfortunate manifestations that carried over into his adulthood. My dad switched jobs a lot. There was a period for a couple years in high school when he wasn't working at all.

Where my dad shines the most is in his humanity. He loves and understands human beings at levels I rarely see others match. He understands why people do the things we do. It allows him to have meaningful and transformative conversations with strangers. My dad possesses the innate talent to influence people to do things they don't want to do. He could sell black spray paint to a polar bear; at least, that was the vision of my dad I had as a kid. It wasn't long into my teenage years that I saw my dad for who he really was: a child victim continuously working hard to make a positive impact in the world.

Growing up, I regularly had a front-row seat to my dad's influence. He went out of his way to buy soft pretzels for homeless people. I've seen him pick up hitchhikers without a care in the world. My dad doesn't fear humans, he fears being unseen. From ages 4–12, he was physically and sexually abused (he even wrote a book about it called *Survived and Thrived*). During his entire childhood, he went unseen and unheard. My dad is making up for lost time and now works in his true passion as a mental health therapist. He went back to school and got his master's degree in his sixties. Way to go, Dad.

Along his journey, my dad made many mistakes. He'll be the first one to tell you all about them. These lessons in transparency and vulnerability were regular occurrences. I saw how people treated my dad. The friends he had loved him tremendously, and I was always intrigued by that. He helped me to learn that by holding in our secrets, we're developing callouses on our hearts. Year after year, our hearts stop feeling much of anything from all the lies and secrets we've told. He helped me to learn there's tremendous empowerment in truth, for we can't hide in shadows when the sun is scorching overhead. He also helped me learn that men can say or do whatever they want; free will is a gift and a curse.

I was young when I realized my dad was just a man made of flesh and blood. It didn't stop me from looking up to him because I was able to look past the decorative allure that we're all so good at displaying. Instead, I choose to stare directly into a person's soul. My dad taught me these skills. He showed me that self-worth should never be confused with net worth—easy for a broke man to say, some would surmise.

But I recognized his deeper lessons. He believed there would be a time I would "succeed," and he wanted me prepared. My dad is an Emotional Warrior, and I wouldn't be able to handle the obstacles in life without him always being there to remind me everything will be OK. Even when I was demoted and wanted to end my life, he reminded me that this happened for a reason and to keep showing up each day, no matter how hard it was. What would I do if I didn't have him in my life? Do you have someone you've taken for granted? Are you missing a parent today?

Growing up, I recognized young how important my mom was to my dad and our family. We would never have survived without her.

My Mama – Robin Bruckner

This book would have never been written if Robin Beyer was never born. My mama is the epitome of grit and determination. When things go sideways, my mom learned how to weather the storm and get through. She would always remind us that bad times never last. She replaced money with home cooking and wonderful holiday memories. She did the best she could while also picking up the pieces in her own life. Our society doesn't like to give moms the benefit of the doubt; moms everywhere are dealing with a lot right now.

I remember seeing my mom cry as a kid and not understand why she was upset. She seemed to be under so much pressure, and I remember thinking that as a kid. Adulting looked really hard. Many days I came home from school to find my mom curled up on the couch taking a nap. I walked in the door from school and her eyes fluttered open. "Hey buddy, how was your day? Can I have just five more minutes, please, buddy?" she asked. "Sure, Mom," I said. She must have been so tired.

My mom is the toughest person I know—the epitome of resilience. She often makes do with what she has and rarely expects anything from others. She gives of herself so that her family doesn't have to be inconvenienced. My mom grew up in an era where many little girls had to learn how to be a wife and mother on their own. Generational trauma was being passed down and few even knew what that was. My mom was married young; by the time she was 23, she was taking care of a newborn son and her two younger brothers much of the time. My mom is the rock for her siblings and parents, and she's the rock for our entire family. Even today, she leads the charge in taking care of both of my grandparents, who are alive and well. How does one person have so much responsibility? Can you relate?

There was a two-year period when I was in high school when my dad couldn't get out of bed. His depression was so severe and he was misprescribed medication. Most days I came home from school, he was in the same spot in bed as he was when I left for school. My mom was working part-time as a server in a local pub to make ends meet. Lindsay and I both had jobs, and life was good for us! Again, we learned early just how gray and messy life is. A positive spirit can carry us through any challenge.

As a parent myself now, I routinely look back and wonder about all the challenges my mom was dealing with. My dad was struggling and couldn't get out of bed. She had a 16-, 14-, and 8-year-old. My mom was working part-time. We couldn't pay our bills. My parents had to literally cry and beg a bank president to loan us money or we may be homeless. That man, by the way, Lynn Matthews, is a retired bank executive who loaned my parents money without any documentation. Lynn watched tears roll down my dad's cheeks and listened to his stories. He simply replied, "I want to help your family. Please give me a couple weeks." My parents never submitted any pay stubs or W-2s. Mr. Matthews saved our family, and he probably has no idea how much he means to my parents.

My mom has earned all of my empathy and grace. She's far from perfect. I see her, though, as the little girl with so much on her plate and the mom fighting like hell to keep her family together and joyful. I love you, Mama!

Seeds of Struggle

The new life transition took a toll on me, and at 12 I told my Sunday school teacher that my dad had a heart attack. I remember her consoling me and how good the attention felt. But I also remember the immediate guilt I felt as I was leaving her room. I was aware enough to know that my lie would soon be uncovered. For me, even at that age, I was highly self-aware and therefore started feeling guilty right away after telling a lie. Throughout my life, guilt would be a common reaction in my life. I bit my nails to soothe myself and now was telling lies to validate myself.

Shortly after the bankruptcy and move, I recall standing on my driveway looking up at the sky. I was 11 or 12 years old. I vividly remember looking into the sunshine and asking God what he has in store for me. I remember it all. Standing there holding a football. Dreaming and believing there was a plan. Several years later, when leaving for Army Basic Training, my mom and I had a conversation where she told me that ever since she was pregnant with me, she had a feeling I would do something special. I remember the validation I felt. This was fantastic news heading into boot camp! I must be destined for great things.

By the time I reached my senior year at Hatboro-Horsham High School (in Pennsylvania), I was playing baseball, running winter track, gaining popularity, and falling in love for the first time. Life was good. It didn't matter that my parents had to sell the family car so they could afford Christmas presents. I didn't care that we didn't have the latest and greatest of everything. We had each other. Love and loyalty. When I meet wealthy people who are unhappy now, I think to myself, *Maybe you chased the wrong thing.*

I was not a good student. I didn't apply myself, and my parents had enough on their plate. No one in my family graduated from college. My options for post-high school activities were limited. My dad is an Air Force veteran. Both my grandfathers served, and so did my uncle. Whether the world selected me to serve or I didn't have any other options, I choose to believe that God had a plan for me all along and I had to learn hard things first.

The Path Toward Human Impact

As an emotional and passionate person, I generally let it all hang out on my sleeves. Today I'm much more stoic and mindful, a product of a lot of personal work and growth. Regardless, I am difficult for some to understand. As a friend recently told me, "You're a layered dude, and sometimes I don't get you." I've heard that before and it used to bother me. I took that feedback personally as I was trying to fit in wherever I was. Over time, I developed low self-esteem, trying to be something I wasn't. I perceived comments like my friends as rejection, and now I understand it's miscomprehension.

As a person who has developed emotional intelligence and practices self-awareness, I often find those traits can be counterproductive in one's life; at least, that's been my experience. I enjoy feeling emotions. I enjoy connecting with others' emotions. Emotions never scare me. I don't have a single memory of being nervous or afraid when someone cries in my presence or wants to have a difficult conversation. Instead, I want to engage. Feeling the emotions of someone in need is my rallying cry.

It's difficult for me to relate to people who bottle everything in. I do my best to demonstrate empathy for people who are unable to be joyful due to their emotional state. For many, they were not raised to express emotions and it's manifested in many unhealthy relationships. For others, they respond to an emotional intervention or awakening—and improve their life!

What kind of human experiences do you think I had as a highly emotional male in the military and policing cultures?

Well, some of the best kind.

And some of the worst.

Exactly as you would expect, and that's perfectly fine.

As a positive person, I always try to be the solution, a light or beacon to help the team accomplish our mission. I won't allow myself to become a distraction or be the conflict that prevents us from achieving special things. I won't be that person. There's nothing more frustrating or disruptive than a disgruntled or selfish teammate.

What I didn't know at 17 was that the military and police cultures are ripe with broken souls.

Rejected by the world? Join the military.

Abused as a kid? Join the police.

Failed out of school? Join the military or police.

Got out of juvenile detention? Join the military and police.

I was one of the healthy ones. My parents were still married, I wasn't abused, and my support system back home was strong. I brought baggage with me, and who hasn't? My baggage appeared to weigh less than many of the men I served with.

The decision to enlist in the military wasn't too burdensome for me. I didn't know who I was as a person and had no aspirations. As my friends were selecting colleges, I felt the need to keep up. The military was a saving grace to keep moving. Several days after turning 17, I gathered with my parents and recruiter to sign the enlistment paperwork. I remember sitting in my parents' family room seconds after signing and thinking, *Well, at least I won't be working at a gas station.* That was my standard. Low-hanging fruit. Few talked about visions or goals back then. Maybe people did, but I did not have those conversations in my world.

I would have plenty of opportunities for vision boards and bold goals later. First, it was time to keep moving and lay the foundation. Complacency and standing still were my enemies. Over the next eight years, the Army kept me moving. I went to basic training (boot camp) at Fort Benning, Georgia, home of the U.S. Army Infantry.

Call to Action

So, there is my childhood in a snapshot. If there is one thing I could put my finger on that made my childhood great, it is love. Love endures and transcends our life experiences. My mom loves Christmas. Every year she decorated the house and played Christmas music starting the day after Thanksgiving. We hung out together while we laughed and baked holiday cookies. Who cared that Mama had to fish change out of the car to buy the ingredients? Money doesn't replace love; it only adds to it. There were times we didn't have two pennies to rub together, but what we had in abundance was love. When times get tough, our resilience is activated. It's a lesson to all of us: Focus on cultivating love in your life, and that will probably be enough. I would need to lead with love as I set out to serve others.

Ask yourself the following questions and be intentional with your answers. Write them down if you have to. Read your answers out loud. Gratitude provides a boost to our resilience.

1. What childhood experiences are you most grateful for?
2. What childhood experiences are holding you back today?
3. What would your life look like if you didn't carry all that weight?

CHAPTER III

JOURNEY OF SERVICE

"LEADERSHIP IS ABOUT SOLVING PROBLEMS. THE DAY SOLIDERS STOP BRINGING YOU PROBLEMS IS THE DAY YOU HAVE STOPPED LEADING THEM. THEY HAVE EITHER LOST CONFIDENCE THAT YOU CAN HELP OR CONCLUDED YOU DO NOT CARE. EITHER CASE IS A FAILURE OF LEADERSHIP."
~ GENERAL COLIN POWELL

SHARK ATTACK

It was August 20th, 1998, and my recruiter arrived at my parents' house at 4 a.m. I still remember walking out my parents' front door, jubilant. I was so raw that I had no idea what to expect and probably had a big smile on my face.

I flew from Philadelphia and landed in Georgia a couple of hours later. I was fortunate to be on the plane with another young man from my same home county. We didn't know each other but would end up becoming good buddies. When we arrived, a gruff staff sergeant picked us up and didn't say a whole lot. He told us to get onto the bus. There were about twenty-five of us who arrived in Georgia from various destinations. The bus ride from the airport was about forty-five minutes. It was eerily quiet. Whenever one of us said something that was too loud, we heard, "Shut your mouths!" Although foreign to me then, I found that using respectful candor in fluid situations has tremendous benefits. On day one, though, I didn't understand what was about to happen. We were about to be eaten by land sharks.

We spent several days at the processing center before going to our units. The processing center was a depressing place. I was eager to begin my new journey, and the clock didn't start until we arrived at our training unit. As I sat in the bunk with nothing but time to kill, my brain was in overdrive. I was terrified of the road unknown. The processing center was my first experience of "hurry up and wait." Hundreds of young men are sitting around all day in uniform, just waiting.

And waiting.

"Soon," the duty sergeant would say.

No one ever had a firm update, yet with each update we were led to believe we would be leaving for our units "imminently," as we liked to say in the military. It was good leadership, I guess. Don't lie to the troops and leave them feeling hopeful.

Check and check.

Still, it was a lonely time, and as a social person, I looked for people to connect with. The beauty of boot camp is that everyone is generally in the same boat. We even looked the same with matching uniforms and shaved heads. If there were ever environments for strangers to come together and accomplish hard things, the military has hundreds of years of experience to know this is the proper manner to train soldiers. I was 17 years old and had to develop into a soldier. Constructing a soldier from a boy is not easy work, and no one prepared me for the road ahead. It's best that we don't know the challenges in life because taking knocks as they come is the only way to build resilience. If we could prepare and plan for every season of pain, we would never truly suffer, a necessary element to building resilience.

Three weeks—twenty-one days—after I arrived at the processing center, we boarded a bus with everything we owned. Our life rolled up neatly into two Army green duffel bags. My stenciled name on my duffels resembled the lettering on circus foot lockers and bandwagons. It was perfect for me. We began to catch rumblings of the impending "shark attack," a ritual where the drill sergeants passionately greet their soldiers as they arrive at their new unit. The greetings aren't intended to be tidings of joy; rather, they prefer to say hello in painful ways.

As our bus pulled up, I couldn't take my eyes off the crowd standing at the drop-off location. There were about twenty drill sergeants and officers standing there with scowls on their faces. Each one filled their Army uniform like a pro baseball player—professional, fit, and all business. Their Smokey the Bear hats could barely contain their personalities. Loud but purposeful. Firm but fair.

The bus stopped, and there was a split second of silence. The senior drill sergeant in the company, who was not a yeller, boarded the bus and calmly said, "Grab your duffels and get off the fucking bus now." He didn't yell, but I recall feeling how serious he was. I had absolutely no idea what to expect; I was 17 and naive. It was in that moment when my ass lifted off the bench seat of the bus that I thought, *Shit, what did I do?* There comes a moment in any scenario when the situation becomes clear. The drill sergeant's look, tone, and manner summed up what discipline still means to me today. There was no ambiguity.

"Move your ass!" was heard repeatedly.

The noise was deafening as we exited the bus. All the drill sergeants were screaming at the top of their lungs. They were providing us with conflicting orders, and we were running into each other. It was chaos—controlled chaos. I learned another lesson in what would become a lifelong education: the world is messy and hard. The better we can handle difficult things and tune out the noise, the better chance we have of winning. I learned very fast that winning for me as a young infantryman meant surviving. My peers back home were focused on passing college exams. Winning for them was getting good grades. I was learning how to shoot, move, communicate, and kill.

Coming from a fast-food joint and a grocery store, being trained on how to kill for a living was something that would surface for the rest of my life. The human brain isn't fully developed until 25, and at 17, I was developing a mindset to kill.

By the end of boot camp, I went from 140 to 165 pounds. I was faster, stronger, and, most importantly for me, more confident. I came into the Army with a strong work ethic, and the drill sergeant cadre further developed my "never quit" mindset. For the first time in my life, I started to stand out. It was like a drug, and I wanted to mainline it.

I was identified as a future leader, something I had never heard before, and it felt good to have leaders pour into me.

Can you think of a time when others invested in you?

How did it make you feel?

Did you tell them how grateful you are?

Are you currently able to pour into others?

If so, what are you doing to help them?

If not, what is stopping you from paying it forward?

Blood rank

It was a beautiful day in the Pacific Northwest. The sun was extra friendly that day, and there was a calmness in my life. I was at peace and proud of my achievements. This time in my life was when I was most confident, and my personal shame was the lowest. The trauma of serving in war and policing in communities was on the horizon, yet I didn't know it that day.

The men were fired up; all eyes gazed upon me. My platoon sergeant, a burly and lovable man from Minnesota, was standing in front of the formation staring at me with a big, cheesy grin. My best friend, Fernando Santos, was smiling but more stoic. I could tell how proud he was. In the formation were several young men I trained and mentored. They would end up doing special things in the military.

That day, though, was about me. I was promoted to sergeant.

At 20 years old, I had been in the Army for three years and was coming into my own as a leader. I already had the official title of "team leader" and had three young soldiers on my team—Ryan, Eddie, and Zack. As the promotional ceremony commenced, I knew my life was going to change as I committed myself to study leadership and mastering it in real time.

After the sergeant's chevrons were pinned on my lapels, the custom of "blood ranking" the new sergeant took place. I was excited and nervous to partake in this custom. The tradition called for me to line up and remove the metal backings from the chevrons on my lapel. One at a time, all senior ranking non-commissioned officers (NCOs) each got a crack to strike the chevrons into my upper chest. Each "pound" was followed by a firm handshake and congratulations. Nothing I did in my 21 years in the military and law enforcement made me feel more connected to my brothers and our collective mission than that ceremony. The bloodstains on my neatly pressed camouflaged uniform shirt were the crescendo of three years of hard work and commitment.

Nando

The most special part for me was having Fernando there. He was getting promoted, too! It was a special day for us. Nando was two years older than me and carried himself like our much older big brother. He was mature and humble. Nando was a first-generation Mexican American and salt-of-the-earth guy. We were best buddies in the unit. He was the Alpha team leader, and I led the Bravo team. We both came from Korea and led with compassion and vigor. We bonded immediately over our sense of humor.

I arrived at the unit at Fort Lewis, Washington, in January 2001. On the first night I was there, Nando came to my barracks room and introduced himself. He knocked on my door in a series of annoyingly brash knocks; they startled me. I didn't even have time to say, "Come in," when the door flew open and Nando walked in. Nando walked into my barracks room like he lived there and said, "Hide your shit, the Mexican is here." I broke out into a loud laugh and introduced myself back. Nando had such a knack for breaking down communication barriers and connecting with people at a basic level. We hit it off instantly.

Nando was a husband and father. I was single and still trying to figure out who I was. For the twenty months I worked with Nando, he helped me develop more during that time than any other period of my life. I needed the positive example. Starting at 20, with Nando's influence, I began to build a strong foundation of good habits to become a highly effective leader.

Nando's best traits were his humility, honesty, collaboration, and positivity. His confidence was also off the charts and in the best way possible. In my life today, at 42, Nando is the most down-to-earth man I've met and the most confident. Think about that for a second. At 22, he routinely said, "I love you guys," and created a culture in our platoon where teamwork was more important than individual merits.

A storm was brewing

As a new sergeant I was expected to execute duties that didn't just benefit my squad. As a sergeant in our infantry company, I would have ancillary duties added to my normal responsibilities, and I loved all the work and responsibilities. I enjoy being dependable and purposeful. Our company had about 130 soldiers, and my first official act as sergeant was to perform charge-of-quarters duties, also known as CQ. CQ is a 24-hour post in the barracks and is designed to ensure there is always someone on duty at the barracks. The shift started at 6 a.m. and ran until 6 a.m. the following day. Truthfully, CQ is a glorified babysitter to make sure things don't get out of control in the barracks. I imagine their duties are like an RA in college.

My 24-hour shift went from 6 a.m. on September 10, 2001, to 6 a.m. on September 11th, 2001.

Ft. Lewis, Washington, is in Pacific Standard Time. As 5:30 a.m. was approaching on September 11th, I was fading fast. Twenty-four hours is a long time! Physical Training (PT) began at 6 a.m., and some soldiers and leaders were beginning to arrive for the day. At around 5:45 a.m., my buddy Victor from the infantry company next door ran into my barracks and said, "Did you see what happened in New York? A small touring plane crashed into the World Trade Center." By this time, many soldiers had arrived for morning formation.

Not thinking anything was wrong, I finished completing my duty log, preparing to be relieved by the next CQ. Our first sergeant then came down the hallway from his office with his usual power walk. Standing much taller than my 5'7" body, he only smiled when something was funny and only yelled when he was angry. He had combat experience, uncommon for pre-9/11 soldiers, and was an intimidating man who commanded respect. At least, that's how my 20-year-old self remembers him. He was an infantryman's dream leader.

As he walked past me in the hallway, he looked straight ahead and said in a loud but controlled tone, "We're under attack, men!" I didn't even know what he meant. A bunch of us followed him to the dayroom. I stood behind him a few steps as he turned on the TV. I was intently watching his reactions just as much as I watched the news coverage. I was curious to know what he was thinking. Perhaps it was my own fears and anxiety that I wanted to solve. Not long after, I would learn.

There were about twenty of us in the dayroom watching the television. Many more were scampering in the hallway and outside in the parade area where we held formations. I imagine we looked like ants after someone disrupted their anthill. There was tension in the air for sure. It was now after 6 a.m. as we watched the coverage in real time. I'll never forget those moments for as long as my brain remains functional. We gasped as Flight 175 crashed into the South Tower right in front of our eyes, followed by a large fireball. I'll always remember the first sergeant turning around and walking out of the dayroom. He was stern but calm and simply said, "Get ready to pack your bags, boys. We will be fighting those motherfuckers."

What motherfuckers? I thought. *What does the first sergeant know?*

I was young and inexperienced. I didn't know who Al-Qaeda was.

The emotions floating around in me initially were confusion and fear. I knew my life was suddenly on a different course. That's how fast life moves. Nando was a different story. He was quiet. Stoic. We worked that day, and instead of going home to his family that night, he asked to stay in my barracks room with me. I had my own room as a sergeant with a set of bunk beds.

I bought a six-pack of Bacardi Silver malt beverages and snacks. We stayed up all night and watched the coverage on television. We barely talked.

Nando and I were both old souls. Reflection and deep talks were normal for us. We pondered in our own ways just how much life was going to change. Fernando was married and had three kids then. I couldn't believe what was on TV. I was heartbroken for my fellow Americans. I was getting angry, too. I had been training hard for three years to fight the enemy. I enlisted in the late 1990s, when it was a peaceful time with a bustling economy. I never actually thought I would have to deploy my skills and training, and that was on the horizon.

That night, however, Nando and I sat in silence as 20- and 22-year-olds watching the news. I looked over and noticed a single tear rolling down his cheek. Nando loved America and represented the best values of this country. He gave so much to America, and he did it faithfully.

Time moved on as she always has. Life doesn't stand still. Nando and I went our separate ways and remained friends. Our military services would lead us both to Iraq, but in separate units and at different times. I was discharged from the Army upon my return home from Iraq and pursued a career in policing. Nando remained in the military, serving the United States faithfully once again in Iraq in 2007 as I was in the police academy back home in the Philadelphia area.

LOSS & HOPE

As the weeks and months passed following the terrorist attacks on September 11th, America began to look different. The brief solidarity started to fade, and spirited debates on the looming wars dominated the news. It's what the new America was. Not much has changed since.

On August 2, 2007, my good buddy Fernando Santos was killed by an IED in Iraq. Lost in his wake are his wife and four kids. I didn't bury the lead with this information because how Nando died paled in comparison to how he lived. I could have started by telling you that Fernando Santos died in a sweaty Army uniform on the side of the road, surrounded by sand, blood, and trauma.

The ugly truth that keeps me up at night is that I miss the hell out of Nando. His loss is a scar that will never fully heal. He was an amazing man, and I am often reminded of his virtue whenever I see a politician make a self-serving deal or a police/military leader betray his/her friends for the sake of their own career. Nando remains with me, like an angel sitting on my shoulders. He guides me and keeps me straight. In return, I'm showing him that we are doing big things just like we always knew we would. That Mexican American kid who grew up poor in San Antonio, who barely anybody knows, is going to make primetime with me, and I can't wait to imagine his smile when that time comes.

He may have died bloody and sweaty on a plot of sand in the desert sixteen years ago, but I will do everything I can to make sure Americans remember who he was and what he stood for. I remember my buddy Nando by how he introduced himself to me. I recall his big smile. When I was homesick, he was the one I could talk to. When I needed help with tactics, he was the expert to guide me. Becoming a man isn't the easiest thing to do, and Nando was the kind of man I wanted to be.

Kind. Hardworking. Humble. Funny. Likeable. Selfless. Honest. Relentless. Loyal.

Twenty-two years after serving together and sixteen years after America lost one of the good ones, I still think of my friend Fernando every time I tell a teammate, "I love you." I resist emotional malaise by connecting and being social with my fellow soldiers and cops. In cultures where emotions are frowned upon, I welcome them with open arms because Nando showed me how effective the love of a teammate can be. Human connection is life-changing and saving.

I rely on Nando's influence tremendously when I'm in my own season of darkness. He demonstrated to me before I could even drink alcohol in a bar how to lead with love while wearing a uniform. I still carry those lessons with me, and I will do my part to give Fernando's ghost the legacy of immortality by living the best life possible and helping as many people as I can.

Thin Blue Line

During my eight years of military service, I received an informal education on organizational culture and leadership. I was in eleven separate and distinct Army Infantry units. In the units I served in, there were new company commanders that came in every two years. Generally, every twenty-four months, the outgoing commander is rotated out for a new commander. This prevents corruption, ineptitude, and unhealthy cultures. The military cannot afford to have disruptions. New ideas and often a vastly different vision can be both beneficial and harmful. Same personnel, new skipper (baseball reference for the team's head manager). That's eleven different personalities. Eleven different upbringings. Eleven different ways of managing stress. Eleven different ways of being human. Eleven different times we had to learn the mindset and ethos of the new commander. Do you know what always changed and looked different? The company culture.

After the Army, I joined a local police department—thirteen more years and three different chiefs of police. Three more different company cultures. I quickly learned the differences between military and police cultures. While they require similar mindsets to perform our duties, I saw many cops approaching police work like it was the military—friends and foes, allies and enemies. Heck, I did too! It's easy to forget that the people we sometimes treat as the "enemy" is our citizens, our brothers, sisters, neighbors, and community members.

I have many positive and rewarding memories of my thirteen years serving my community. We saved neighborhoods from open-air drug markets, tracked down violent offenders, and even helped people kick their drug habits. I was hired five months after I got married. We had all three kids while I worked at the police department. I grew from a boy to a man at the police department. It will always be a place I revere.

I was promoted to detective in four years, and my partner Nick and I formed the Street Crimes Unit, an undercover unit in our small community that focused on the violent quality of life of crimes like narcotics, robberies, assaults, and burglaries. My chief at the time, Robert McDyre, was a former narcotics officer and wanted to clean up our town. He cared a great deal about the community outcomes, like his predecessor.

His predecessor, Chief Joseph McGuriman, was a gentle and kind man. He hired me in 2008 and retired nine months later. I was his final hire, and after his retirement ceremony, he approached me and said, "My best hire was my last hire." He gave me a soft smile, which made me feel welcomed and engaged. I was loyal to our agency; they were going to have to carry me out in a body bag if they wanted me to leave. I was passionate about building a life and career there.

Eleven months after being hired as a police officer, I enrolled at DeSales University in Center Valley, Pennsylvania. My wife, Kristen, is a schoolteacher, and when we met at 25, she already had a master's degree. She was the head cheerleading coach at

DeSales, and I looked up to her tremendously. She inspired me to push myself and encouraged me through her examples that I had more inside of me than I was showing. It's the power of influence and modeling virtue. I wanted to keep up, so I decided to get a college degree. For people that know me personally, going to college at that time was the furthest thing from my mind, largely because I heard the comments over the years that "Chad's not a good student" and "College isn't for Chad" and believed them!

Now, as a new police officer and husband, Kristen was helping me develop into the man I am today. I enrolled in 2009 and took one class at a time until I graduated with a bachelor's in criminal justice in 2015. I didn't get good grades, and I was the first Bruckner to graduate with a college degree (my dad and sister have since attained degrees). Kristen was there with Lucas and Malia, and my parents. At 34, that was the proudest I felt in my life. I felt joy when I got married and my kids were born. Getting my college diploma after a lifetime of thinking I was a moron was the first step in understanding there's so much more to my life than what others place upon me.

Would you believe that I kept going, taking one class at a time? I graduated with a master's in digital forensics from DeSales in 2020. The irony is my great friend and partner, Nick Oropeza, was also going for his master's degree then. I started before him, but since he was taking two classes at a time, he was scheduled to finish before me. I was struggling to write my thesis and sat on it for almost a year. I was mentally preparing myself to say, "I did the coursework for a master's but don't have the actual degree because I didn't write my thesis."

Nick would tell me weekly, "I'm coming for you, bro."

Iron sharpens iron, as it reads in the old testament of the Bible, and without Nick and I pushing each other, who knows where we'd be? In a department of about thirty officers, there were only three officers who had master's degrees: Nick, Matt, and myself. Nick and I achieved everything possible to take the next steps on our journey and be promoted to sergeant. I was getting my degrees to put myself in the best position to lead as chief of police someday. I was open with my intentions because I didn't want to be sneaky. I'm an open book and subconsciously placed targets on myself. I had no idea that behind the scenes, some of my brothers and sisters would work against me. That's how naïve I was—blinded by my passion for serving human beings.

Less than a year into my role as a patrolman, I started to experience hurtful comments from colleagues. I had a senior officer on my squad who was out of shape and didn't have much confidence. Instead of encouraging and mentoring me on how to become a great police officer, he ridiculed me for how I approached the job. I was confused and trying to learn the job, which can be challenging. I had a big smile and wanted to make a big impact. I also had big dreams and healthy confidence. That seemed to offend the personal nature of this officer, and he projected his insecurities onto me. It got so bad I had to tell my squad leader and then go see the chief.

"Do you want me to discipline him?!" my chief said firmly.

He didn't seem to favor this officer and sounded hell-bent on not having me tainted by lazy and unconfident officers. Having his support meant the world to me and gave me the confidence to keep serving in the manner I know how. Looking back, though, I see how being emotionally imbalanced as a chief can have catastrophic consequences. We simply cannot make things personal as leaders, and so many do.

After Chief McDyre retired, the department promoted his replacement from within—someone I knew very well because he was my supervisor for six years leading up to his promotion.

Insecurities + ego + ambition = toxicity

Soon after getting promoted from patrolman to sergeant, Sergeant Matthew Pathe was friendly and helpful toward me. He was charming at times, collaborative, and kind to me. He came from a big city department and seemed knowledgeable about drug enforcement, which was my passion. Looking back, I realize now that he didn't have as much drug experience as he alluded to. It was a lesson that I would have to learn the hard way. Some people are ambitious and will do and say whatever to advance their careers. I was being gaslit and didn't know it.

Manipulation is a talent and skill that, without guiding values, can be used for bad. Truthfully, Kristen did not like Sergeant Pathe when she first met him. She has a great ability to read people, and unlike me, she is not emotional. She read Matt correctly on day one and even told me. Yet, I would have to endure pain to learn what Kristen knew right away.

As Sergeant Pathe started mentoring me, I found great comfort in having him in my corner. He routinely reminded me that I was a great detective doing great work. He advocated for me and would even stand alone to defend me and push for me to get other opportunities.

How lucky was I to have a leader care for me like that? It was not long until we became good friends.

During this new time as a Detective, I was working for a different sergeant, Jason Winder, who was the supervisor of detectives. Jason did not have much drug enforcement experience. He was kind to me as well, but he sat in a position that Matt wanted, and he is a tactician. I've seen how strategic Matt can be; he is willing to get his hands dirty in political mud. It seemed that it was a criterion in the area I worked. I rarely met a chief who was leading from the front, and the ones who did were trashed by other chiefs. Jealousy reigns supreme. Sergeant Pathe is an envious person by nature, and instead of celebrating others performing well, he routinely trashed people in what I only assume was a direct assault on his insecurities. Sergeant Pathe is a schemer who's willing to do and say things I'm uncomfortable with to advance his career. I imagine this is how many politicians operate—they take hostages.

Matt wasn't a bad supervisor then, but I was in a game where I didn't know the rules and was unaware of the pitfalls. If this was a game where there were winners and losers, I was never supposed to win. It's essentially what is happening in the United States today; most Americans don't understand the deep state occurring in Washington and therefore won't be able to compete fairly. Knowing the rules, understanding political landscapes, and developing healthy boundaries are all things I struggled with, and for someone like Matt, it was a recipe to manipulate and take advantage of.

Over the next six years, Matt and I worked together every day. He was a friend and mentor. There were times I told him, "I love you, brother," and personal moments when he disclosed immoral things that, because I'm a good person, I won't say in this book because they would cause him personal harm. I won't stoop there, and besides, in his heart, he knows exactly what he's done, so there's no need to go further. I kept his secrets and lies as a good friend does. It's actually what our culture expects.

In 2017, I turned down a county detective position largely because of Matt. A county detective position is the crown jewel to many police officers I worked with. It's the reward of a long career of service; and a goal for some cops to end their career. I declined the position because I'm loyal and we had more work to do at my agency. I don't jump at the bright and shiny things that make some feel good about themselves. I largely know who I am and what I want out of life. I always remember Matt giving me a big hug and saying, "Thank you, brother." It was one of the best feelings I experienced inside my own agency. It affirmed my decision was the correct one.

In 2018, our former chief retired, and the search for the next chief was on. For the past year, I watched Matt scheme behind the scenes to set himself up for chief. Simply applying and competing for the position was not enough. Matt worked hard to leverage his position as detective sergeant. He used the work Nick and I did to bolster his leadership skills. In reality, there's not much Matt taught us. He was skilled at making it look like he developed us, but he was interested in coming out for search warrants or drug buys because of overtime compensation.

Matt approached me and asked me to help him make a video for his chief application packet. We came up with the idea to do a mock press conference. I set up the shoot and got the logistics squared away. Matt worked on the script and we came together to shoot this short film. It came out spectacularly and Matt sounded great in it! After Matt scored #1 on the chief selection process, he approached me and hugged me. He said the selection committee loved the movie, and I felt so much pride to have a direct hand in helping Matt get promoted to chief. After Matt got promoted, the detective division went out for beers to celebrate. We all felt like we earned the promotion. I felt that same feeling in the military and it made sense to me. I recall Matt seeming off balance that night, like we were prouder than he was. He seemed stressed by it all.

Very soon after Matt's promotion, the detectives noticed something was off. Matt started distancing himself from us. He would not attend social events anymore with us and started treating us differently than he did before. The divide was tangible.

The eyes of a great white

As I entered 2020, I was hoping for an uplifting year, and I would soon learn that it would be a historic year. My personal shame was growing for many reasons. I was unhappy with my work. I was having mental and emotional health issues. Looking back, I could have embraced those uncomfortable moments to build resilience. Are there times when you've wasted moments to build your resilience? Are you in one of those moments currently? My wish for you is to run into the pain. I know it will hurt, but with each blow, the pain lessens. This is how we build higher levels of resilience.

The year of 2020 was an eventful year in the news as well as my personal life. I was in the middle of my demotion back to patrol and the sting was still strong. I was struggling to process the betrayal, and the reality set in that Matt was never a real friend. I fell victim to his manipulation and gaslighting. As the reality set in it my situation, whatever boy remained in me was gone. My childlike positivity and light were gone.

I will never forget the look in Derek Chauvin's eyes when he killed George Floyd. I was on duty at the time, patrolling the community, when I got the notification on my phone. I pulled into a school parking lot and immersed myself in the news of the day: police killed a man in Minnesota. As I watched the video over and over again, I was flooded with my own experiences. War memories, police experiences, all the unkind things that ever happened to me. Those emotions all hit me in my police car. It's the first time I said aloud, "Policing is broken."

Chauvin had the look of someone I recognized. Burned out. Stressed beyond recognition. I imagine the face I saw of someone murdering a fellow citizen was much different than the night Chauvin had his badge pinned on his chest all those years earlier. Watching George Floyd die on camera in front of the world to see was a defining day in our career as police officers. I then watched police executives, legislators, and elected officials try to make sense of it. Leaders pointed fingers at others, and few inside the profession wanted to take responsibility.

Instead, I watched my chief of police speak at a rally in support of diversity and inclusion; only to Black Lives Matter once the cameras stopped rolling. Many police leaders were talking out of both sides of their mouths, and three years later, we haven't advanced the cause far enough. Daily I asked myself, "Are we trying to fix this or not?" It has been three years since reform was needed, and stakeholders continue to point fingers at the community, elected officials, and the media. The truth—the ugly truth—is that the blame lies within our profession. That's when the concept of moral injury hit me like a truck.

Despite so many police officers laying their lives on the line for others, there were countless police leaders who did not seem to want to fix the problem. They are content with the status quo, and that caused me a significant moral injury.

Moral Injury

According to the VA, moral injury is characterized by guilt, shame, and self-condemnation one feels after being exposed to traumatic and stressful environments where people perpetrate and fail to prevent events that go against one's moral and spiritual beliefs.

I had been laying my life on the line for others since I was 17; it's all I knew professionally. I couldn't fathom how some leaders actually worked against making things better for the common good because it didn't benefit them personally or financially.

The military culture is a rough culture, at least when I was in from 1998–2006. As a highly emotional male, I'm susceptible to emotional ambushes, which I've experienced many. I define an emotional ambush as an emotionally intelligent person with dishonorable intentions who play on the emotions of their victim to gain compliance. Clinicians may diagnose this person as a narcissist. My first emotional ambush was in the Army when I got to my first unit. I had just turned 18 and was halfway around the world. I was so inexperienced I couldn't even identify who was an ally and who was a wolf in sheep's clothing.

When I was 18, my first Army leader was ten years older than me. He was carrying a lot of unresolved personal childhood trauma, and he was one of the most charismatic individuals I've met. He was a classic narcissist, and the inexperienced me would have to learn the hard way exactly how and what narcissists do to take advantage of people. I carried that guilt and shame with me for twenty years. He would not be the last narcissist with unresolved trauma I would work for.

I came to the policing community after eight years in the military. At only 27, I was a seasoned and combat-tested leader. I came into the police department with a healthy sense of confidence. I was eager to share my leadership knowledge and also eager to learn from the experienced leaders in the agency. I was in for a rude awakening. The juxtaposition between the military and policing leadership cultures was significant.

In the military, the culture was to have our troops get the first crack at welfare and recreation. Leaders sacrificed and did everything last. At least, that's what I did. In the policing culture, seniority plays a huge role. Leaders often take vacations on the days they want over their junior officers. How did this become an acceptable standard? More importantly, why hasn't this policy, which is clearly in violation of leadership best practices, changed? The year 2020 helped me to realize that despite being incorrect or misguided, many police leaders choose to lead in the way they are despite knowing it's not the best practice.

Shortly after the George Floyd riots of 2020, I was serving as a patrol shift supervisor on a Friday night in June 2020. The weather was warm and there was a large group of approximately 30–40 protestors standing in the middle of the road, slowing down traffic. They had a bullhorn and were holding signs. They were causing a scene, and it was by design. They wanted to be heard. These protests and rallies were common in the aftermath of Floyd's death. This is just one month after the riots in Philadelphia in which my squad was dispatched in riot gear to protect a Target store. On this particular night, the same squad was working when this new group of protestors was standing in the middle of Main Street, partially blocking traffic.

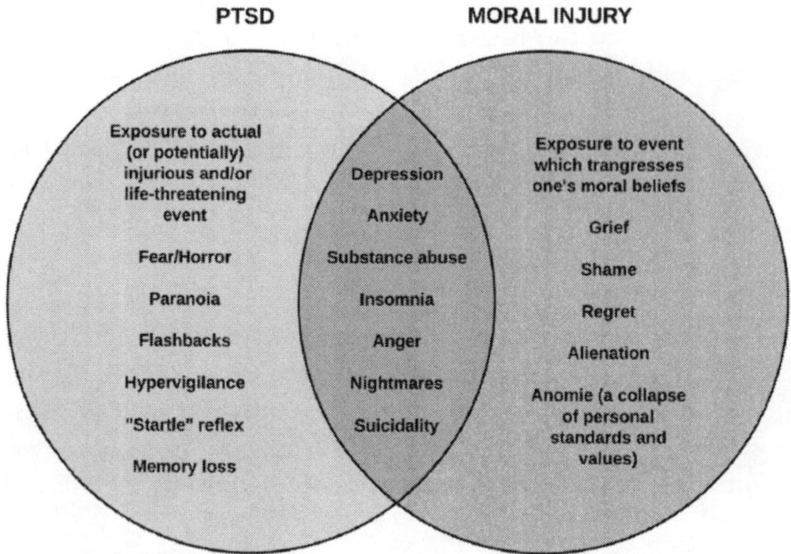

Chief Pathe contacted me as the shift supervisor and said, "I just got a call from Council. Get those assholes out of the street."

"Chief, what if they don't cooperate?" I asked.

"I don't care if you rip 'em out of the streets. I want that road cleared," he replied sternly.

Use of force was not an option and everyone on the squad knew it. When I briefed the plan to the squad, I knew not to throw Chief under the bus. Regardless of my personal feelings about him and his leadership, I've been around long enough to realize complaining about someone would not be helpful to the mission. Plus, I understand how quickly morale plummets when the leader loses hope and bashes senior leaders. I simply told the squad that I was going out alone to meet with the group so we don't agitate the group. I advised the squad that we would not be using force unless we were being attacked, plain and simple. I don't care how loud someone gets; I was trained and prepared enough to study actions and behaviors, not words.

I went out to the middle of Main Street and met with the protest leader. She was angry and rude to me even though I was asking to have a conversation with her. I was patient and collaborative. Nothing about that encounter was about me or the police department. In my mind, we were two citizens trying to come to an understanding. Guess what? We didn't come to an understanding. They did not honor my requests to move out of the roadway. I thanked them for their time and walked back to my patrol car.

Instead of taking action, I chose to do nothing. I sat in my car and observed the group. With each passing car honk, they felt validated. Within thirty minutes, the sun began to go down and rain moved in. Without me having to do or say anything further, the group left the roadway and dispersed.

What would have happened if I had followed my chief's orders? I think we all know what would have happened. I called Chief Pathe afterward and updated him. He replied something to the effect of, "You're right, we shouldn't have removed them forcibly. Thanks for keeping us out of hot water."

Keeping Chief Pathe out of hot water seemed to become a course of conduct the longer we worked together. I really didn't care because I always wanted the organization to "get it right," and I didn't care who was "right."

Taking Hostages

I'm going to describe the man who fills the chief uniform. This would be his draft report if he was a professional athlete:

Positives: Ambitious, intelligent, and resourceful.
Negatives: Immoral, twists the truth for personal gain, unethical, not a team player.

Being open and honest in the workplace has many positives. The appropriate vulnerability of police officers among each other and the community has tremendously healthy effects on interpersonal relationships. The flip side to that is when we're working with fearful and paranoid teammates, the vulnerability we display can be used against us. I had some hard lessons to learn about trust and loyalty. I barely could utter the word "betrayal" because it's so contrary to my core values.

Very soon after Chief Pathe got promoted, the relationship started to change. He began treating all the detectives in a cold manner. I'll never forget walking up the hallway only weeks after he got promoted and saying, "Good morning, Chief," with a big smile on my face, being playful. Chief Pathe walked by and barely cracked a smile and replied, "Good morning, Chad." It was in that moment that I should have known, but my blind loyalty and good nature would be challenged in a big way.

Can you think of a time when you were bamboozled? How did you feel? What was the fallout? How did you recover?

Shit or Get off the Pot

By the middle of 2020, I finally came to the realization that our agency was only getting more unhealthy. Moreover, I pushed past my denial to admit to my inner self that I was in an environment that was selfish, and that's why the arrows were now coming after me. During many midnight shifts on patrol, I would look up at the moon and ask God, "There has to be more for me, right?"

Those desperate questions and waiting on signs from above would further lead to my hopelessness. I went from making things happen to waiting for things to happen. How, though? Organizationally we stopped becoming forward-thinking for the greater community; and began the ugly business of being transactional.

I really don't care that policing has become a harsh intersection for citizen interactions, but I prefer that imposters presenting to be caring and inclusive only to engage in self-serving efforts to be exposed for what they are: unhealthy contributors to a noble profession.

I found a way to be tough on crime and lax on human issues. It was the perfect recipe to hold people accountable *and* selflessly serve the community. I don't care if someone needed a hand picking weeds; I took great pride in being able to be both versions of a police officer. To me, it was no different than being a husband or father. I prefer to be collaborative, engaging, and kind, and I also can protect my family with vigor and violence if need be. That's how I approached police work. Should this be the standard?

By July 2020, Kristen and I decided to start investigating the possibility of retiring early from law enforcement and forging a new path, as terrifying and hopeful as that sounded.

ACT II

WINTER

CHAPTER IV

HOUSE OF CARDS

"A SOCIETY GROWS GREAT WHEN OLD MEN PLANT TREES WHOSE SHADE THEY SHALL NEVER SIT IN."
GREEK PROVERB

The next two chapters were the hardest for me to write. I'm not a complainer so it's hard for me to sit intentionally and be critical. I knew I had to try to properly explain how things really are in many police departments in the U.S. Please bear with me as I focus on hard truths about what police officers and communities are facing.

Why Focus on Character When We Can Curate Our Reputation?

As John Wooden once said, "Be more concerned with your character than your reputation because your character is what you really are, while your reputation is merely what others think you are." The ugliest truth in this chapter is that many executives and elected officials have worked hard to strategically curate their reputation at the expense of their character, and everyone in our teams sees it. Ethics and morality are required ingredients for healthy cultures.

When police departments build their cultures on a weak foundation, they tend to struggle in all areas, from team member morale to overall performance. Without a strong organizational culture, team members may not understand their role within the department or know how their work contributes to the community's success as a whole. This can lead to confusion and miscommunication, ultimately leading to lower productivity and decreased morale. Additionally, a weak culture can also prevent strategic leadership from taking hold, as the lack of established values, norms, and expectations creates an environment in which innovation and creativity cannot be nurtured. In the end, this lack of clarity and direction can lead to an underperforming agency that is unable to stay ahead in its community. If you don't know if your culture is unhealthy or not, evaluate every member of the police department. Do they have free reign to serve according to their talents? Are police officers routinely going to training and developing themselves? Are leaders and executives spending time with their officers or others who don't add value to the agency? Are you allowed to freely express yourself? Can you be honest with your leaders?

Leaders who must tell their teams they have an open-door policy most likely are ineffective leaders. Effective leaders cultivate trust, and teammates don't need to be told there's an open-door policy; they just know based on the strength of relationships. We often want to hear stories about the boss sleeping with the secretary as an indication of unhealthy work culture. However, those are sensational cases. It's usually the subtle and consistent subterfuge that eventually takes down an organization.

The term "house of cards" refers to something that is structurally unsound and easily collapses. It metaphorically alludes to a house of cards that has been constructed from playing cards, which is inherently unstable given the way the cards are balanced. It often applies to a situation or scenario that is delicately balanced and easily disrupted. An organization built on a house of cards looks unsustainable and is very fragile, although from the outside it may not be immediately apparent. An organization built on a house of cards may appear outwardly strong, but if one card gets removed, the entire structure will collapse, often with catastrophic consequences. The organization will lack depth, be difficult to maintain and grow, and have limited long-term success. Additionally, poor decision-making is likely if the house of cards is the foundation of operations, contributing to the fragility of the structure.

Departments built on a house of cards are one crisis away from everything being exposed. When we create cultures based on optics and perceptions, we've only created a thin veil of perfection. As we know, perfection is an illusion, and we come into work on Monday already playing from behind.

If police agency executives do not lead with ethics, morale within the agency will likely be significantly affected. Team members will sense that there is an atmosphere of corruption or dishonesty and may not trust leadership to make ethical decisions. This will likely lead to decreased morale, productivity, motivation, and overall commitment of the members of the agency. Additionally, it will be more difficult and exhausting for team members to work in an environment of mistrust and uncertainty. When this occurs, retention typically suffers as high-performing members of the agency transition to other opportunities. In the case of my former department, two experienced officers have left without full retirement in the past three years in an agency less than 30 officers. I believe there will be more.

In record time, the chief transitioned the agency from an institution of merit to a place where talent fades. Even as officers struggle mentally and emotionally, organizations would rather pile on the good cops than hold the bad ones accountable. The current detective sergeant at my former agency is not qualified for her current role, yet she is actively working on being promoted to lieutenant. It's rather delusional behavior, and leaders who don't have self-awareness, the good men and women in that department, will suffer. The blind ambition to attain more titles and validation only erodes the culture. Instead of we, it becomes acceptable to lead with me. Truth seems to be the enemy as leaders twist narratives to satisfy their ambition. and that scares me for police officers. Executives who don't lead with courage, passion, and fairness end up taking hostages inside their own agencies. The culture, perhaps strong outwardly, is a sham designed to keep the heat off the executive. When police executives allow politics and career ambition to cloud their judgment, organizational culture will erode, and depending on the specific agency, it would be rather quick.

Intersection of Policing and Politics

The relationship between politics and policing in America has been complex and often contentious. For centuries, politics have had a strong influence on police operations and on the way policing is conducted in the United States. This influence can be seen in the way police forces are funded, the way police departments are organized, and the way police interact with the public.

In the past, local governments have had complete control over their police departments, creating a system of patronage and politics. This patronage allowed local politicians to use police personnel for their own political benefit, often creating tensions between elected officials and police officers themselves. This deep politicization of the police has resulted in an environment where there is often a disconnect between the top brass and the street-level officers.

Unfortunately, the politicization of police departments has also led to corruption and incompetence within these departments. Political pressures have forced police to take sides between elected officials and the people they serve, creating a system where their loyalty is more to the politician than to the public or the officers they lead. Political patronage has also led to the selection of police personnel for political purposes rather than for effectiveness and qualification.

Additionally, the rise of powerful police unions in the 1980s and 1990s has greatly exacerbated the problem of politicization. Unions demand more resources for their members and fight back against attempts to hold officers accountable. This is especially true for police use of force cases, which can often be excused due to the weight of police unions and their influence over municipal authorities. I understand the need for police unions, and like any other institution, it comes down to who is leading these unions.

I was in our Police Benevolent Association. I didn't know what benevolent meant when I got hired. According to Webster's, benevolent is defined as "an organization serving a charitable rather than a profit-making purpose." When I learned the meaning, I was happy to sign up. I donated $5 every week for about ten years to help people in the community. In reality, we spent most of that money on contract disputes and attorney fees. Where's the benevolence in that? Around 2017, I left the union. I was the only officer not in the union and was happy to be following my gut. I think there is something morally inappropriate to identify yourself as a benevolent association when we barely conducted charity work. I talked with many police officers across America, and they reported similar experiences. We have largely become a fearful profession where service has died. Now, we lead with the policy manual and evaluate decisions on liability instead of potential impact.

The militarization of police forces in recent years has further contributed to the politicization of policing in America. I believe the militarization of police departments has more to do with mindset than equipment. Highly successful agencies require high-caliber equipment to perform and meet the demands of the community. AR-15s and tactical gear are necessary to keep a nation and communities safe. Where we have fallen—mightily—is the treatment of our citizens. Our citizens are not the enemy. They are our brothers and sisters. As policing evolved into the "law enforcement profession," we often alienate the very people we're tasked with defending. We made it "us versus them." I can have an AR-15 slung across my chest and talk with a citizen because I can smile, make eye contact, ask them how they're doing, and build a relationship. If citizens start seeing us again as humans first, we can usually work through conflict together so that it doesn't stunt operations and future relations.

Overall, politics have had a dramatic impact on policing in America, creating an environment where there is often a disconnect between the public and the police, where resources are misallocated due to political influence, and where accountability is increasingly difficult to maintain. As such, if police in America are to regain the public's trust and move toward effective and equitable policing practices, the politicization of police forces must be reversed.

Criminal justice agencies must remain nonpolitical to ensure the impartiality and fairness of the criminal justice system. Any sort of political interference can have a detrimental effect on the trust between communities and police officers, as well as the integrity of the criminal justice system. If the actions of police and other criminal justice agencies appear to be influenced by political bias, it may undermine the respect the public has for these agencies and potentially result in a breakdown of law and order.

When I retired from policing, I met with a council person at the municipality I served. I tipped him off to what's happening inside the department and no action was taken. I don't blame this council person. The system is fractured and that's how bad eggs slip through the cracks. It's ironic that communities want bad cops off the department; more of the blame lies at the feet of the chief executive and the elected bodies who hire these bad eggs. Yet, we throw the officers under the bus to save embarrassment or organizational ridicule. Police culture permits eating each other alive on certain occasions. It's rather a bully culture where cliques, authority, and information rule.

Foundations

Building criminal justice agencies on a house of cards creates an unreliable foundation for its success. A house of cards is an inherently unstable structure, and an organization built on such a foundation will lack resiliency and stability in the face of changing conditions. As the environment shifts, this house of cards will crumble and will be unable to withstand any kind of external stressors we face today. This can create a chaotic workplace environment where mistrust, fear, and poor communication can take root and ultimately lead to the downfall of the company. With no trust or foundation to build upon, the company is no longer able to identify and anticipate the needs and interests of its members and other stakeholders, which can cause it to quickly become irrelevant.

The house-of-cards culture, where everything looks good from the outside but is toxic on the inside, is the primary reason bad cops are disciplined and good cops leave. It's no different than an abusive and toxic household. From the outside, it may seem fine and dandy, but when you pull the curtain back and pay attention, we will see if we choose. Some elected leaders don't want to see, and that needs to change.

Police Executive Appointments

The most important hire any police department will make will be its chief executive. All things flow from the chief. It's absolutely critical that municipalities consult with regional thought leaders from the profession to assist in the selection. One of the major issues I've seen is how elected officials make these selections here in Pennsylvania, and few actually know what makes a good police chief. It's easy for candidates to highlight themselves and curate a reputation necessary to get these positions, even if they manipulate information or people to get them. The system has created a power play for the position. Chief candidates attach themselves to organizations or people who can help them. For some it becomes a pursuit of ambition, leaving behind the cops who never went to college and don't have much support at home. Those cops are the ones usually hurting citizens and going to prison for it. Morale, welfare, wellness, and culture all become expressions of the chief's ideology.

Don't have an empathic chief? Then we would expect the officers to become the same way.

Don't have a virtuous chief? Then we can expect that officers will also stray from their values.

Don't have a healthy chief? Then be prepared for the mental and emotional health of the department to suffer.

Broken leaders do not develop good teammates; they destroy them.

Chiefs don't just lead their officers; they lead their families too. Each selfish and unhealthy decision begins to erode the officer's ability to weather storms. As information becomes currency, officers outside of social cliques have stress added to their already full plate as they have to wait on information and opportunities. Here's the thing in toxic cultures: merit really doesn't matter. It's not about performance and service anymore; it's about fear and control. I guess a logical question to consider is: Who hires police chiefs to begin with? Elected officials with no policing experience make the final decision. In the middle are stakeholders, some with special interests. This is where corruption takes place and political pipelines can be formed. Even local governments and communities have now befallen to duplicity.

Most elected officials are not qualified to hire police chiefs because they lack the technical and professional expertise that is necessary to effectively evaluate the qualifications of police chief candidates. The process of selecting a police chief requires expertise in areas such as law enforcement, personnel management, and related operations. Elected officials do not typically possess these necessary qualifications. Additionally, allowing elected officials to appoint police chiefs could undermine public confidence in the fairness of the police department's hiring process and lead to allegations of political favoritism in the selection process.

Preschoolers with Guns

Working in a toxic workplace isn't much different than daycare. Immaturity, secrets, misinformation, kiddie games, etc. All these factors can have significant negative impacts on your physical and mental health, not to mention your career. Unfortunately, many people find themselves in this situation without even realizing it. When people say, "Give me an example," they may be waiting to hear a story about the brash boss sexually harassing women as common signs of a toxic culture. However, it's often the sneaky and distracting maneuvers that hurt us without us even knowing. Sure, the womanizing boss is a problem, but that's low-hanging fruit.

I'd like to draw your attention to the tacticians who don't operate according to values. These leaders move about the organization, consistently evaluating how matters affect him or her. My former chief was given bonuses for how much he reduced overtime costs. Lowering costs and expenses is a good thing; few would argue that. However, he took the overtime budget down by over 70% in his first year as chief. That level of brash and rushed decision-making comes with consequences.

First, numerous officers count on that overtime to pay bills and support their families. If an executive is going to take it away, it must be a collaborative process. My former chief values money tremendously and would fight tooth and nail if anyone tried to take money out of his pocket. Yet, he had no problem taking money away from officers so he can get paid. The municipality paid him a bonus from the overtime money that would have gone to his officers. Some would say that's theft. I call it poor and selfish leadership. With social media and technology exposing poor behavior, the brash boss has been replaced by a boss who is leading a psychological warfare campaign against his people.

Psychological warfare is the new brash boss. It's the subtle subterfuge from those charged to care for us that hurts the deepest and most long-lasting. If a stranger walked up to us and gave us the middle finger, most of us probably would laugh it off since we're not emotionally invested in the relationship. Now imagine a scenario that I think is very common where young people get hired together at a police department or any company and become close friends. As the years go by and the friendship builds, so do their career ambitions. As promotions become rarer, the fight for achievement and recognition intensifies. In unhealthy organizations, once-close friends become bitter competitors. Behaviors change for some, and their character can be unrecognizable.

Competition forces some in the department to forge new allies with those they were once foes of. Scheming begins to become routine. Isolation happens more frequently. Confusion sets in and roles are blurred. In the end, the unhealthy culture they were in broke their friendship, and they were ignorant to prevent it. Bad systems ruin good people. I hope this book can help heal many relationships.

Organizational Betrayal

Organizational betrayal is when an organization betrays the trust of its members. This can be caused by a number of reasons ranging from malfeasance and negligence to discrimination and workplace harassment. Organizational betrayal can have a major impact on the overall functioning of a police department, leading to decreased trust, further conflict, and lower morale between officers, leaders, stakeholders, and the public. Additionally, it can lead to increased complaints, litigation, and difficulty in recruiting new officers.

Another sign of organizational betrayal is when officers leave before their retirement date. After I left, we had another officer who sacrificed six years of pension time and left before being vested. Reasons don't matter, and that's the point. Healthy organizations retain talent; unhealthy ones don't. All police officers want is to be fully supported by their organizations, through the good and bad. Don't we love our people enough to do that?

Many police officers don't even realize they're in a toxic culture. It's important to be able to recognize the signs of a toxic work environment because then you can take steps to protect yourself or move on to a healthier work environment.

What follows are some of the most common signs you may be working in a toxic workplace.

1. Bullying or Harassment

The most obvious sign that someone is in a toxic workplace is that they experience bullying or harassment from coworkers and/or superiors. This could be verbal bullying, physical bullying, sexual harassment, or any other type of offensive behavior. If you find yourself in a situation where you feel like you can't stand up for yourself or you're made to feel uncomfortable by others, this is a red flag that things are not okay in your work environment. If this happens to you, journal the incidents to keep an accurate record of the events. I kept a list of Chief Pathe's behaviors to protect myself.

2. Poor Communication

Poor communication is often an issue when it comes to a toxic workplace. This could be the lack of communication about tasks or cases, or there could be a lack of clarity when it comes to expectations. It could also be a lack of communication about promotions, contracts, etc. If you feel like you're not receiving the information you need to do your job effectively, then this could be a red flag that you're in a toxic workplace. Poor or miscommunication is a necessary ingredient for toxic workplaces. It's how they thrive.

3. An Atmosphere of Unhelpfulness and Competition

When working in a department with a toxic work environment, teammates may feel that they are in competition with each other instead of working toward a common goal. Employees may feel that their colleagues are unhelpful or uncooperative and that everyone is always trying to get ahead. Few outside of the department would see this, but a culture that cultivates this environment puts a lot of stress on officers and other staff members. This type of culture does not help the officer feel safe and trusted, core elements to developing resilience.

4. Low Morale and Lack of True Teamwork

A lack of morale and teamwork can often be a sign of a toxic working environment. Officers may feel like they are not trusted or supported by their colleagues or superiors or that their ideas and goals are not respected. This can make it difficult to work in a cohesive and effective manner. I can't tell you the number of times I sat in the squad room listening to officers talk very negatively about other officers openly in front of others.

When this type of behavior occurs routinely and is engaged by the majority of the department, it is nearly impossible to feel safe inside the police department. Every action is scrutinized and judged. The stress on the street was often for me less than that inside my own agency. If officers are engaged in negative talk of other officers (really, humans!), then they're not "team players." Teammates—*true* teammates—don't talk behind their brothers' and sisters' backs. True teammates don't tell lies to one another. True teammates never betray each other. Colleagues do that. Peers do that. Sadly, friends even do that. But a true teammate, whether at work or in life, would never do any of those things. There's your measuring stick.

5. Unfair Treatment

Unfair treatment is one of the most common signs someone is working in a toxic workplace. This could range from preferential treatment for certain individuals to outright discrimination. If you feel like you're constantly being treated unfairly, this could be a sign that things aren't as they should be in your work environment. You shouldn't have to make sense of somebody's actions. If we're supposed to be fair and kind to one another, then when someone is not kind to you, that's their problem. Leaders can't take hostages by making personal and biased decisions. It's just that simple. We see this more and more in the news, whether it be judges exceeding their reach because they "don't like" what happened or politically motivated witch hunts by both sides of the aisle. There are police executives who rule like kings instead of influence like leaders. How did that happen?

It's not "your" police department, it's the communities. That credit belongs to the men and women, not "you."

Professional Coaching and Self-Development

Executives in policing are not like CEOs in private business. I'm the CEO of two small businesses and have much more perspective now of what each takes, and I think the profession has done itself a disservice trying to brand ourselves as "professionals." Policing is a noble profession; we don't need to compete or compare with private industry. Chiefs don't need vision boards. They don't need fancy degrees and constant training; personal development is done at home. We have professionalized the job to the point that chiefs seem to spend even less time with their officers than in previous generations. The men and women in uniform need leadership. They need to know their leaders care, not some bureaucrat scheming for the next spot. Remember, police officers are not working in a mail room or sunning themselves on the beach. They're putting their lives on the line, and some officers are literally dying in the course of performing their vocation. Close your eyes for minute and think about that. Their job could cause them death, and for the majority of police officers, they're changing no matter what as a result of their profession. Don't we owe them more? Shame on the executive who forgot where they came from.

A toxic workplace can be difficult to deal with, but it's important to be aware of the signs so you can take steps to protect yourself. If you feel like you're experiencing any of the signs mentioned above, it's best to reach out for help. We most likely all have someone in our life we can talk to, even if it's an older neighbor we trust. Be vulnerable, open up, seek input, and challenge your perspectives. Ignorance is not an excuse anymore. Don't suffer in silence like I did for much of my thirties—reach out and get the help you need.

I have a professional coach because I understand I can't lead alone. Leadership is challenging, and I learned to surround myself with people who will do the following:

1. Hold me accountable
2. Always be truthful
3. Places the mission before ego
4. Cheer me on
5. Value the relationship

Solutions

The best method of identifying police chief candidates depends on the needs, expectations, and goals of the community and police department. Common methods include conducting a nationwide search, recruiting from within, assessing internal candidates through performance evaluations, or creating a review panel to evaluate applicants. Additionally, public input can be sought from citizens, stakeholders, community organizations, and other law enforcement agencies for a comprehensive range of perspectives.

We ought to reevaluate the processes and metrics we use to identify talent. **Emotional intelligence** can be of great value to a police chief. A successful police chief needs to be able to handle stressful situations with composure and confidence and have strong interpersonal and communication skills. Emotional intelligence allows the police chief to be able to effectively interact with both citizens and officers and help to create a successful and unified team.

Chief Pathe was a hothead who couldn't regulate his emotions and took hostages with his dysfunctional behavior. If chiefs learn emotional intelligence, they can better meet their officers where they're at in their life and career. I created a matrix that recruiters, consultants, and elected bodies can use as a tool to select an executive. There are ten parameters that can be reset to fit the specific agency. The most critical part of this survey is to select ten leader parameters that are important to the department. I chose the ten factors I have learned to be most critical for leaders.

Leader's Assessment Survey (LAS)

Parameter	1	2	3	4
Job Experiences			X	
Job Knowledge			X	
Collaborator			X	
Influential				X
Transparent				X
Virtuous		X		
Impartial/Unbiased			X	
Community Focused				X
Facilitator			X	
Officer Wellness Priority		X		

4 15 12

Sample Demonstration – 31 points

40 maximum points

1 – Low

4 – High

32–40 = This leader is a mindful and thoughtful person of influence. This person leads by example and models proper organizational behavior. This leader is someone who values collaboration, positive feedback, and open communication. They listen to their team's ideas and respectfully address any concerns. They are flexible and open to change when needed. They also possess excellent problem-solving skills and are willing to take risks to make a positive impact. Finally, they have the ability and the confidence to make quick decisions for the good of the organization. This is a leader who inspires and influences. You will build an organization around them and they will always put the organization first. Do not pass up on this candidate.

26–32 = This is a leader who understands the goals of their team and is poised and confident in achieving them. They are patient and thoughtful, taking the time to consider all the angles rather than making hasty decisions. At the same time, they are decisive and bold when it is necessary, backing up their decisions with sound reasoning. They understand the strengths and weaknesses of their team and employ each one effectively. They are strong mentors who support their team, fostering trust and respect. This leader is self-motivated and enthusiastic, setting an example for the team to follow. This is a leader who is dependable and reliable. This leader has the emotional bandwidth to lead through adversity and still perform at a reasonably high level. Collaboration is a strength for this leader. This leader will have deficiencies and the maturity to receive feedback and the wisdom to make change.

4–25 = This is a leader who avoids confrontation or decisions because they are afraid of the potential repercussions or conflict. They may put off important decisions and delay important conversations to avoid interaction with their peers or subordinates. They often lack the confidence and vision necessary for strong leadership and instead focus on maintaining the status quo. Cowardice leaders may not be ineffective in accomplishing tasks, but they are ill-equipped for creating an inspiring or motivating environment. When challenges arise, they might work to undermine or criticize their team when things don't go as planned. This type of leader is often uncomfortable giving clear, firm feedback and will instead politely brush off any issues or problems. They may also rely heavily on the opinion of others to make decisions as they lack confidence in their own. If a candidate scores in this category, there is a likelihood that they won't effectively lead in times of crisis.

Call to Action

Close your eyes and imagine for a minute that your police department operated solely on merit. They only advanced officers who earned it. Only those with leadership abilities get promoted. The chief executive is the most moral member of the agency and sets an example for others to follow. This should be a standard, not an outlier.

I further challenge you to reframe the definition of "go-getter." We should not reserve the distinction of meritorious performance solely to how many arrests an officer makes or how popular they are. There are many agencies right now employing an empath, an officer who routinely adds value to the lives of community members. They volunteer to do the extra things that really transcend relationships. Maybe their value isn't as quantifiable. That's not their fault, it's yours! Find a way to find their value. Celebrate them for it. The issue with many executives is that they, too, only think drug work and SWAT calls are sexy. We have glamourized policing and don't invest the resources into other initiatives that may have better community engagement results.

Be unique and different from the agency next to you. Challenge the chief next door by being better. Be OK with receiving criticism and resist falling in line so that you don't make them look bad. You're not making anyone look bad other than themselves. It's up to each of us to lead, and if you find yourself in a spot where you're not leading authentically to your values, then I hate to burst your bubble, but you're not a leader. You're a person occupying a position. Whether you become a leader is up to you, and if you can't even identify yourself as one, that's for your team to decide.

What are you going to do to change your culture?

What is stopping you from making the hard changes?

Write these answers down and hang them on your desk. Look at them every day until you can't stand to look at it any longer. You may not know *what* to do, but you'll start realizing that you must do something.

CHAPTER V

UGLY TRUTHS

"I REMIND MYSELF EVERY MORNING: NOTHING I WILL SAY THIS DAY WILL TEACH ME ANYTHING. SO IF I'M GOING TO LEARN, I MUST DO IT BY LISTENING."
-LARRY KING

"My father told me when I was a little boy that people in authority lie."—Robert F. Kennedy Jr.

This was by far the most challenging chapter to write for me and also the most cathartic. Speaking the truth about a toxic profession I love is hard. Whenever we're truly honest, we run the risk of alienating people in our lives that we respect and love. That is never my intent and certainly was not in this chapter. If we're going to truly evaluate and make difficult changes, every stakeholder must be honest and lead with respectful candor.

The most challenging part for me of retiring early from law enforcement was I didn't leave on my terms. I was forced to make a decision to preserve my health. I would have preferred to stay on the job and continue to make an impact. The ugliest part of this is realizing that my former employer made a catastrophically bad hire for chief of police, and despite me advising an active duty council person about the toxicity and poor human treatment there, it was met with apathy.

We have a leadership and ethics crisis in this country because many leaders lack the courage to do what's right. Despite knowing what the right course of action is, many leaders lack the courage and lead with shame and indifference. Leaders must be passionate, and without vigor, leaders are empty uniforms. This is what policing has become—so little inspiration anymore—and that's directly attributed to elected bodies selecting and hiring ineffective executives. In the past two years since I bought a private investigations firm, I have learned more about the hiring processes and further developed a stance for improvement. In my current role, we conduct background screening for local government officials. We also consult municipalities on their hires. Hiring police executives has largely become political appointments, and that results in executives leading from the brain and not from the heart. This is how we arrived at the recruitment and retention issues. Leaders and politicians want to point their fingers at the media and communities because that's easier.

The ugliest truth is many leaders aren't qualified to influence human beings, and this generational oversight has finally caught up to us. I know many qualified leaders who cannot get promoted within their agency due to "politics" or "poor culture." If we installed executives who understand leadership and are empathetic and compassionate, cultures will improve, morale will rise, relationships with the community will strengthen, and good cops will come back. First, though, executives must admit that they're the driving force behind the problem. Effective leadership creates momentum and covers up much of the bad stuff around our teams. If executives are constantly talking about problems, momentum cannot be generated.

Another ugly truth that many officers report is the paranoia from their chain of command. I experienced this as well. I always put the community and agency first. But, since I was working for someone who put himself first, he led from a place of paranoia. He assumed everyone was trying to take advantage. There are many initiatives I presented to my chief that would have had tremendous benefits on the community, and no other agencies were doing what I suggested. It was shot down, and one time, I remember being laughed at, presumably because it wasn't the chief's idea, or he assumed I was presenting this for personal gain somehow. He is unable to see past his own baggage and it's ruined the fabric of the department, which I know affects the community. Shame on the elected persons who turn a blind eye once they've been informed. Effective leadership is hard, and I guarantee when we bury our heads in the sands to challenging things, they only fester and get worse. Rarely do major human problems just go away on their own. They require human intervention and connection.

Ineffective Leadership

Poor leadership within an agency can have far-reaching and long-lasting consequences. Poor leadership generates an environment of distrust and miscommunication, which can put an entire agency at risk. Poor leadership may lead to inefficiencies in operations, reduced morale, a lack of innovation and creativity, an increase in staff turnover, a decrease in customer satisfaction, poor customer service, and potentially even legal issues.

When poor leadership is in place at an agency, the results can have serious implications. Without a strong and capable leader, staff may become demoralized, leading to reduced performance. Teammates may become disengaged, while lower-level staff may take a more significant role in decision-making and operations. This can lead to a lack of innovation and creativity since staff are not able to suggest new processes or procedures.

Poor leadership can reduce citizen satisfaction. Without a competent leader in charge, service to others begins to suffer. Teammates may become resentful of their leaders for not providing adequate training and support, which can result in poor service and an overall drop in community satisfaction. Teammates may also become frustrated with the bureaucratic organization, leading to a decrease in team loyalty.

Self-serving decisions made by leaders also have catastrophic effects on morale and culture. Leaders engage in self-serving behavior for a variety of reasons, including to increase their power or status, to protect their reputation, or to gain personal financial gains. In some cases, self-serving decisions may be made to promote short-term gains at the expense of long-term success or the needs of a group or organization, or they may be made out of a sense of entitlement or arrogance.

In 2018, we had an officer out with an injury. Chief Pathe, a paranoid and anxious leader, believed this officer was laboring or embellishing. This officer's absence caused a patrol shortage. The chief had each detective take a thirty-day patrol rotation to fill the void. I was a detective then and was certain that he was taking this action in the hopes that we would get upset with this officer and force his return to work.

The detectives had a meeting, and collectively we decided not to say a word to this officer. We recognized what was happening and had to prevent potential problems. Instead, we accepted our thirty-day rotations in patrol without a word. We knew what Chief Pathe was doing. Instead, we supported that officer, and he ended up coming back in a couple weeks, so detectives didn't need to fill patrol shifts. Filling a patrol shift was never the problem; it's how we were being used as pawns for poor leadership.

A few months later, our chief was in the detective's office chatting with me and another detective. When this officer's name came up in conversation, the chief said, "I thought you guys were going to squeeze him to come back to work."

The detective and I made eye contact and did not say anything. After the chief left the office, we couldn't believe he admitted it out loud. Somewhere along the way, he was shown or taught that using teammates against other teammates is the preferred leadership modality. Time and time again, we were putting fires out to protect ourselves. We learned to look out for ourselves.

When the rank and file don't trust or feel supported by the chain of command, all is lost. Poor leadership can lead to legal issues. Without a capable executive, an agency may be more susceptible to litigation. There is a higher chance of errors or missteps occurring without proper oversight, which can create potential legal issues. Chief Pathe has been sued multiple times by his own officers, even within his first year of tenure. How is it even possible that within your first year, you cause enough grief to be sued by three members of your department? Well, it happened.

Many executives chalk this up to leadership or "the cost of doing business." The ugly truth is it's not only ineffective, it's also toxic and dangerous. Police officers are dealing with so much already, and the last thing they need is a self-serving chief making their lives worse, not better. If policing wants to restore nobility and bring recruits back, we must begin by creating cultures in which being sued by your own officers should be a referendum on your performance, not a feather in your cap.

Poor leadership can have lasting and serious consequences for an agency. It is essential for leaders to realize the importance of their role and always strive for excellence. By doing so, leaders can create a positive and effective working environment, thereby resulting in greater success for the agency.

Brain Health

If we're going to change police culture, let's start with creating better language to break down the stigma. Cops and soldiers are used to working our bodies hard. Physical fitness and health are critical to performing and serving. We even enjoy working out. If we must work our bodies to be top notch, don't we also have to work our brains (the most important organ in our body)? I think we *must* if we want to thrive on the job. So, instead of mental health (such an ugly term for some of you, right?), let's go with **brain health**. Doesn't sound as bad, right?

Brain health is an important factor in the decline of police officers, as it can lead to a number of issues that can affect their performance and overall well-being. Stress, depression, and anxiety are all common brain health issues that can have a negative impact on the performance of police officers.

Here are statistics from a presentation made at an Anxiety and Depression Conference in 2015:

- → 75% divorce rate compared to a 50% rate among average citizens
- → 25% alcohol dependence rate
- → 2–4 times more likely to commit domestic violence
- → 2 times the rate of depression
- → Suicide rates of 16.4–18.1 per 100,000 officers
- → 8–11 years shorter life expectancy
- → 80% of officers considered overweight
- → 25 times more likely to die of heart disease

More police officers die every year at their own hands than every other police death combined. We are our worst enemy, not the media or the public. Stress is a major factor in the decline of police officers, as it can lead to physical and psychological exhaustion, which can lead to decreased performance and an increased risk of injury. Stress can also lead to decreased morale, as officers may feel overwhelmed and unable to cope with the demands of their job.

Depression is also a major factor in police officer decline. Depression can lead to feelings of hopelessness and worthlessness, which can lead to decreased motivation and performance. It can also lead to an increased risk of suicide, which is a major concern for police departments. Depression can be seasonal or chronic. Don't wear your depression as a badge of honor, seek help with your doctor and make a plan toward healing.

Anxiety is another brain health issue that can lead to the decline of police officers. Anxiety can lead to feelings of fear and panic, which can lead to decreased performance and an increased risk of injury. Anxiety can also lead to physical symptoms such as fatigue, headaches, and difficulty concentrating. Anxiety is so common within police culture, and we can do a lot inside our agencies to minimize the anxiety that many police officers serve with.

All these brain health issues can lead to decreased performance, increased risk of injury, and decreased morale. It is important for police departments to recognize the importance of brain health and to provide resources and support to officers who are struggling. This can help to reduce the decline of police officers and ensure that they are able to perform their duties effectively.

Police executives must embrace brain health to promote healthy cultures and keep staffing levels at appropriate levels. The job changes every one of us, and we should practice self-care, work in supportive cultures, and be proactive about the family issues that come with serving communities. Police executives need support, too, and just like an airplane oxygen mask, I recommend leaders heal themselves first before trying to help a buddy. Often, our pain prevents us from being helpful.

The ugly truth that many leaders struggle to understand is that they have a direct hand in promoting the brain and emotional health of their officers as well as directly setting organizational culture. If there is a toxic agency, simply gaze at the senior executive, and we will understand why the agency is the way it is. When we study healthy and strong workplace cultures, we will always find strong and present leadership teams. Policing, for generations, has neglected the health and training of officers. I am not surprised we're in this situation.

Chief of Police Selection Processes

Selecting police chiefs has become a political process, and that is the fundamental reason law enforcement is in decline. We have stopped modeling good behavior and leading from the front. Too many executives are concerned about their own contracts and compensation packages. Too many are more concerned with their own career. When leaders focus more on themselves than their teams, all momentum has been lost. The culture is now toxic. Apathy is another silent form of toxicity. I fear too many officers have worked in nothing but apathetic cultures and therefore assume that it's a healthy culture compared to other agencies. Apathy is a dangerous form of toxicity and affects more agencies than we would like to acknowledge.

As a student of leadership and culture, I informed my chief four years ago that he would ruin the department if he continued down this road. He got upset and offended. (I had already been demoted at that point). He was not emotionally prepared to lead an agency and multiple officers have left the department since—*before* full retirement, the worst indictment on a police executive.

As a profession, we don't seem informed or interested in being educated on proper leadership. The primary issue is we have too many police executives, and few of them were developed properly. They're now leading agencies and taking hostages within their agencies. The suicide rate is high and many of them have blood on their hands for how they intentionally and systemically target officers and work to ruin them.

Stigmas and Judgments

Few can eat each other alive better than cops. Some of the most judgmental and broken people I've served with are police officers. They carry so much trauma and shame, and that manifests in unhealthy treatment of their brothers and sisters. Consequently, some of the most virtuous people I know are police officers. However, we're not going to fix this by kicking the can and continuing to only talk about the good. We must have difficult conversations about the bad so we can rip the Band-Aid off and start moving forward. It will require humility and honesty. Not everyone will make it with their pride or careers intact, and that can be scary. We created this ourselves and now don't want to put the work in to get ourselves out of it. The lust for authority has corrupted a once noble and necessary profession. Thought leadership is needed more than ever.

In recent years, the issue of brain health stigmas in the police force has been brought to the forefront of public attention as police departments and brain health experts have begun to recognize the importance of addressing these complex issues. Mental illnesses, including depression, anxiety, and post-traumatic stress disorder, are often too closely linked with the art of serving communities and experiencing the worst of societal problems. This stigma can lead to a lack of access to mental health support and services for officers, even though they are under increased pressure and are more likely to experience traumatic events.

The stigma of brain health for the police is problematic for two key reasons. First, it can prevent officers from seeking help when they are struggling with brain health issues because of the feared negative consequences, such as being labeled as weak or crazy. This creates a vicious cycle where officers are more likely to suffer in silence and be less likely to share their situation and access the help they need. My former chief labeled an officer "crazy" in order to ostracize him—and it was effective. In 2019, this officer went through a negative work event, and Chief Pathe began using language like "crazy" when referring to this officer in attempts to smear the character of this officer. In reality, this officer is one of the most virtuous people I know in public service. Chief Pathe is not the only police leader who does this. Do you see how we ended up here as a profession?

Second, the stigma of brain health for police officers can create a culture of fear, where officers may fear that if they seek help, they will be seen as unfit for duty. This can lead to officers being reluctant to come forward with their issues, meaning their brain health may suffer in silence. As the compensation packages rise, many officers who once never thought they'd earn the kind of money they are may not get help because they don't want to jeopardize their careers. I know many police officers who make over $130,000 with a high school diploma, and their spouse doesn't work. As their brain and emotional health has worsened from their job, they find themselves cheating on their spouse or abusing drugs and alcohol when they would have never condoned that behavior otherwise. How do cops violate their own personal values? Unresolved trauma, in my belief. Our brains get rewired from the trauma of the job and the toxicity within our agencies. Good men and women change. We must understand these changes and come to their aid. Imagine a broken officer right now serving in a toxic culture. Do you think they're hurting? Maybe they just helped a citizen at the same time they're dealing with a divorce. This is what officers experience every day.

Fortunately, more awareness is being raised around brain health stigmas in the police force and many police departments are taking action to provide officers with the help and support they need. Brain health training, peer support networks, and counseling programs are being implemented in many police departments to ensure that officers can get the help they need.

At the same time, it is essential that societies continue to work to break down the stigmas surrounding brain health in police officers. Education around brain health issues and mental illness can help promote a safe and supportive environment for officers struggling with brain health issues. This will help to ensure that officers can access the help and support they need without fear of judgment or punishment.

Childhood Trauma

The ugly truth that few inside policing want to acknowledge is the level of untreated and unresolved childhood trauma that many police officers are carrying around and leading with. Unresolved trauma in our lives has catastrophic effects on our health and interpersonal relationships.

According to a 1994 research poll conducted on 558 law enforcement and mental health professionals, 19.6% of law enforcement professionals reported childhood abuse, while 29.8% of mental health professionals did (Follette et al., 1994). If these numbers are consistent, which I believe to be true based on my commitment to studying people and human behavior, then we have a mental and emotional health crisis on our hands. One in five police officers have *reported* childhood trauma, so it's reasonable to assume those numbers may be higher.

Here's what I found interesting: People who experienced trauma are more likely to enter professions involving trauma. Broken people working to make the world a better place! It's a beautiful thing. However, if those broken people don't heal and recover, then they end up becoming monsters who take hostages and ruin lives. If more police leaders healed, they would be more joyful and their agencies would flourish.

First responders and veterans are often exposed to traumatic events, which can lead to post-traumatic stress disorder (PTSD). PTSD can be caused by a variety of traumatic events, including childhood trauma. For first responders and veterans, the effects of childhood trauma can be particularly pronounced and can lead to a variety of mental health issues.

Childhood trauma is defined as any experience that causes intense fear, helplessness, or horror. This can include physical, sexual, or emotional abuse, neglect, or witnessing violence. Research has found that childhood trauma can have a lasting impact on an individual's mental health and can lead to a variety of mental health issues in adulthood.

For first responders and veterans, childhood trauma can lead to an increased risk of developing PTSD. This is because they are already exposed to traumatic events in their line of work, and childhood trauma can make them more vulnerable to developing PTSD. Studies have found that childhood trauma can increase the risk of developing PTSD by up to three times.

Childhood trauma can also lead to a variety of other mental health issues in first responders and veterans, including depression, anxiety, and substance abuse. These mental health issues can be further exacerbated by the stress of their job, leading to an increased risk of burnout and decreased job performance.

Childhood trauma can also lead to an increased risk of suicide among first responders and veterans. Studies have found that individuals who have experienced childhood trauma are more likely to attempt suicide than those who have not experienced trauma.

The effects of childhood trauma can be long-lasting and can have a profound impact on the mental health of first responders and veterans. It is important for first responders and veterans to be aware of the effects of childhood trauma and to seek help if they are experiencing any mental health issues. Treatment options such as therapy and medication can help first responders and veterans manage the symptoms of PTSD and other mental health issues.

Narcissism

Narcissism is a personality disorder that stems from a deep pain we carry around. When we are in pain, we tend to focus on ourselves. As we focus on ourselves, we are working to make ourselves feel better. As celebrity shrink Dr. Drew says, narcissists have a deeply wounded core, and they are moving about the world trying to feel important and necessary in order to satisfy the deep pain and trauma they're feeling. Dr. Drew opines that unhealed childhood trauma leads to a developed version of an adult who grows up engaging in behaviors, often harmful and toxic, in attempts to protect themselves from an empty feeling they have inside. There are many narcissists serving in the military, healthcare, government, and law enforcement, and if we bring attention to the issue, we can help them heal. These broken souls could develop into healthy leaders if they're accountable for their behaviors and they're serving in a culture where toxic behaviors aren't permitted.

Unmeritorious Promotions

Police leaders may surround themselves with less-than-qualified leaders in order to maintain control over their departments. By having a less qualified leader in a position of authority, they are able to have greater control over operations and make decisions without having to consult more experienced or qualified personnel. Additionally, having less qualified leaders in positions means that their potentially weaker skills and knowledge can be easily overlooked in favor of the leader's own. This allows the leader to make decisions in line with their personal agenda and objectives rather than having to consult outside expertise. Over time, this leads to an unhealthy organizational culture and poor retention. In other words, our agencies become a graveyard for talent.

Here are the most common *bad practices* used daily in police agencies across the United States:

1. **Making decisions based on stereotypes, outdated beliefs, and gossip.** Police leaders may decide to assign officers to certain types of calls or neighborhoods based on negative biases that have been firmly ingrained in policing models for generations.
2. **Discouraging officers from reporting wrongdoing and misconduct.** Police leaders frequently turn a blind eye to allegations of wrongdoing and misconduct by officers in order to avoid liability, which is a dangerous and unethical practice.
3. **Failing to hold officers and leaders accountable for their actions.** Police leaders may allow officers to get away with serious misconduct, such as using excessive force without any disciplinary action, creating a culture of impunity.

How many leaders in your police department have free reign to do what they want?

4. **Not adequately training or supervising officers.** Police leaders may fail to provide adequate training or supervision on the proper use of force and de-escalation techniques, resulting in officers who are unprepared to interact safely with the public.
5. **Not evaluating or monitoring officer performance.** Without evaluating and monitoring officer performance, police leaders are not able to identify problem officers, develop plans to help them improve, or take appropriate action when necessary.

The Trinity: Organizational Culture, Leadership, and Wellness

Wellness and leadership are critical to organizational culture because they help to create a positive work environment that is based on mutual respect and collaboration. A healthy and happy workplace is more likely to foster innovation and productivity, while an unhealthy and unhappy workplace can lead to a lack of motivation and low morale. When leaders promote wellness and lead from the heart, they create a culture where employees feel valued, meaning that they can focus on their job without worrying about health concerns. In addition, leadership provides a shared vision for the organization and sets the standards for behavior. It provides a strong foundation for team members to build upon and is essential for the success of the organization.

The ugly truths can be corrected with an honest reflection on what we're doing today and analyzing where we came from. Truth is the only way we repair. Hiding from the truth only fosters distrust in the department. Let's get into the meat and potatoes of this book!

CHAPTER VI

LEADERSHIP

"A GOOD PLAN VIOLENTLY EXECUTED TODAY IS BETTER THAN A PERFECT PLAN NEXT WEEK."
-GENERAL GEORGE PATTON

Leadership vs. Supervision

Supervision is the action of supervising someone or something, while leadership is the practice and action of influencing a group of people or an organization toward a common goal. Leadership is more than being a taskmaster; it's a skilled art that takes concerted focus and discipline. Leaders cannot be self-identified; they must earn that title from the teams they lead. Otherwise, they're simply supervisors.

Effective leaders understand human behavior and therefore rely on the importance of modeling proper behavior for their teams. Human beings are social creatures, and we learn from others and, as a result, either develop good habits or poor ones. Just like a parent inside a home, leaders who model good behavior for their teams increase the likelihood that their teams comply with agency policy and directives.

So many leaders and executives fail to understand that if they are taking shortcuts, so will their teammates. If parents use drugs and alcohol routinely in front of children, there is an increased likelihood that kids will use substances than those children who do not see their parents use substances. It's a logical and reasonable understanding of human behavior. If parents pray in front of their children routinely, we increase the likelihood that our children will be spiritual. Leaders and parents should never lose focus on the flip side.

When leaders and parents model unhealthy and dysfunctional behavior, the culture begins to be impacted. When leaders treat teammates to different standards, individual officer identity begins to suffer. When leaders begin to conduct backdoor channels of communication, the lack of transparency leads to distrust. When distrust forms inside an agency, loyalty is harder to come by. Cliques begin to form, and many inside the organization will silo themselves in efforts to protect themselves. Fear breeds secrecy. Personnel will begin to eat each other alive, and much of it is done in secret. Gossip takes hold, and lies permeate the culture. Much like in America today, in-fighting takes hold and distracts the ordinary officer from the real problem, a toxic culture.

Here's the primary concern every chief of police and commandant should never lose sight of: the senior executive in the agency is the sole determiner of agency culture. The agency will go as she/he does. If agencies want inclusion, empathy, strong communication, and influence, then stakeholders would be wise to identify markers and metrics they can use in the selection process to identify the right candidate. We must evolve from the old way of thinking where cops who led their agencies in arrests or are on the SWAT team are the preferred candidates for chief regardless of if they demonstrate a high degree of leadership skills.

Effective leadership can create tremendous momentum in the organization and in the lives of our teammates and their families. Let's talk about the problems first so that we can talk about solutions.

Influence vs. Authority

Influence and **authority** are two different forms of leadership. Authority is based on a positional power where one has the right to make decisions and demands, while influence is based on relationships, where one uses their relationships to gain commitment to an idea or action. Influence encourages people to take ownership over their decisions, while authority sets boundaries and assigns tasks.

Accountability is required in leadership roles, and if we want to deploy influence to gain our teams' compliance, we must own all of our actions as leaders. Accountable leaders own their behaviors and have strong relationships within their teams.

Accountable leaders are generally exceptional leaders because they're good at fostering trust and loyalty. Being an accountable person best leads to high performance, less conflict, joy and fulfillment, and healthier relationships.

Influence is the preferred compliance method because it works better in highly competitive and complex modern agencies. Influence encourages people to stay engaged and allows for creative thinking in problem-solving. Authority restricts people's autonomy and creativity and can create an environment of fear and distrust. Influence takes more commitment and patience from the leader. You won't see teammate buy-in right away, and leaders must be consistent. An inconsistent and/or disingenuous leader is nothing more than a boss—and someone you have to learn to manage.

Persistence & Consistence

If you have ever served with a highly effective leader, then you already know one of their best traits: how routine they are. Effective leaders understand that to have influence in their teams, they have to be action people. Slogans painted on the walls inside the agency are disingenuous if the department culture doesn't back it up. True leadership is showing up every day to deliver an honest effort. It's through that concerted effort to influence others that by itself carries a lot of influence in our teams. Officers, like any employee, observe the actions of their leadership. Hypocrisy is sniffed out quickly. Cops are trained observers and know bullshit right away. Yet, many cops in leadership roles are too overwhelmed to notice how ineffective they actually are.

The best leaders don't have all the answers but are there every day with their teams working through the day. Close your eyes and imagine an ambitious parent who works sixty hours a week. They're too preoccupied with their own success to realize they're failing their primary role of mentoring, coaching, and preparing their children to live a virtuous and successful life. Instead, they buy their kid an Xbox and wonder why they grow up to be insecure and unprepared for the realities of life. Parenting is leadership; you'll never be a great parent if you're not spending time with your children routinely. They need you just like cops need their leader to support them in their careers. Similar to being a kid, cops experience many challenges and would probably crush them all with a little persistent and consistent engagement from their leaders and executives.

Chad's Leadership History

I was promoted to sergeant at 20 at Fort Lewis, Washington. It was September 1, 2001. I was hand-selected for promotion. I had leaders identify me for a leadership track and then invest heavily in me. I've been to a lot of leadership development training—they're great for education and enrichment—and practiced the art of leadership 24/7/365. I was promoted alongside my good buddy Fernando Santos. Ten days after we were promoted, we stood silently and watched the Twin Towers fall on a television in our barracks dayroom. We were new infantry sergeants whose entire existence was to train, lead, communicate, shoot, move, kill, or capture. That was our order of operations, and we recognized in that moment that we'd soon be putting those skills to the test.

Fernando was killed in action on August 2, 2007. This loyal Mexican-American, who was a father of four, died as a result of a roadside bomb in Iraq. Nando was the best leader I served with. At 22 years old, he routinely told his soldiers, "I love you." He hugged and affirmed his men. He held his men accountable, too. He molded young men coming from all over the country, many from broken childhoods, into lethal and compassionate American fighting men.

Few American or Mexican citizens know Nando and they will never know how much he cared about this country. He cried on 9/11. I watched his anger manifest into focus. He inspired me tremendously, and I still carry him with me today. I was 20, and he was 22. He seemed like he was 45 to me. Still today, I look back and marvel and how mature and self-aware he was. He knew what he could do and what he couldn't. The level of care he had for his men outweighed his tactical knowledge, and Nando was one of the finest battle minds I was around. He routinely kept lieutenants on their heels as he seemingly always knew the operations plan better than the leaders who created it. Privately, Nando was a family man. A humble man with salt-of-the-earth vibes. I have many memories of eating dinner with his family and watching him play with his sons. It made me miss my dad. He was proud of his family. We would drink beers in my barracks room after work and he would tell me how proud he was to have a family and be present for them. Nando's family was his whole world.

When Nando was killed, I was nearing graduation from the police academy. I was also engaged and due to be wed a week after graduation. I had a lot of positive momentum going. It was a hopeful time for me. Guys from our old unit started texting, and we set up plans to attend Nando's funeral in San Antonio. Nando's death crushed me. He was a better man than I was, and he had four children.

The survivor's guilt that followed his death weighed me down. The issue for me was I didn't want the unwelcomed and unpleasant distraction. My life was going great. I had an amazing woman agree to marry me and a career that seemed perfect for me. Nando's death ripped open my baggage. So, I wrote a letter to his family and respectfully advised them I wouldn't be able to attend his funeral. Missing Fernando's funeral would eat at me slowly over the next decade.

Effective Leadership

Effective police leadership is responsible for setting the tone for how officers interact with the public. Police leaders must ensure that their officers are respectful and courteous when dealing with members of the public and that their interactions are conducted in a manner that is both professional and appropriate. Police leadership must also ensure that officers are properly trained in de-escalation techniques and that they are aware of their legal and ethical responsibilities when interacting with members of the public.

A significant difference between effective and ineffective leaders is that effective leaders typically model the behavior they want from their teams. Leaders who model proper behavior and those who don't lies in the impact they have on their team. Those who lead by example set a positive tone and inspire respect, trust, and loyalty, while those who neglect proper behavior can breed mistrust and a lack of motivation or commitment from those around them. Leaders who model good behavior create an environment of accountability, high standards, and team development which ultimately leads to greater success. Leaders who don't model the behavior they expect from their team create an atmosphere of mistrust and disorganization and can have long-term damage.

Leaders are also responsible for providing support and guidance to officers in difficult situations. Police leaders must be able to provide officers with the resources and support they need to effectively handle difficult situations, such as those involving mental health crises, domestic violence, or other high-stress situations. Police leaders must also ensure that officers have access to the necessary resources to help them cope with the emotional and psychological stresses of their job.

Executives are responsible for ensuring that junior leaders are leading and serving at the highest levels. Junior and mid-level leaders are the backbone of police agencies and require leadership, coaching, and mentoring to reach peak performance. How many executives are spending daily time with their officers mentoring them to lead and preparing them for the dark seasons?

Junior and mid-level leaders must also ensure that officers are held accountable for their actions. Without accountability from every single officer, especially leadership, agencies will never be able to reach their maximum potential. In fact, many agencies celebrate themselves simply because they have zero or few internal complaints and no internal investigations. That's not success; that could very well be fear. I know of an agency in a county near me that has over forty internal investigations going on with approximately 100 officers. There's no fear there—they demand accountability.

The problem there is the municipality hired the wrong chief to lead them. Leadership is very hard, and many police executives weren't prepared to handle the hard. They want good times and smooth sailing. Many will work hard to curate a culture where it's mostly window dressing. Conflict and discomfort are the enemies for them, when in reality, the only way to lead effectively is to roll up our sleeves, tell our teammates hard truths, lead by example, never quit, put others first, and embrace the things that scare us. That's leadership, and for many police leaders, they're unwilling or, more commonly, ill-equipped to do so.

Police leaders must ensure that officers are held to the highest standards of professional conduct and that any violations are appropriately addressed. Police leaders must also ensure that officers are properly trained in the use of force and that they have the necessary resources to effectively handle difficult situations.

Proper leadership is essential for ensuring that police officers are able to effectively serve their communities and protect the public. Police leaders must be able to provide guidance and direction to officers, set the tone for how officers interact with the public, provide support and guidance to officers in difficult situations, and ensure that officers are held accountable for their actions. Without strong police leadership, police officers would not be able to effectively serve their communities and protect the public.

Servant Leadership

Servant leadership focuses on the empowerment of the individual, which can result in improved morale for law enforcement and military personnel. This in turn can lead to improved performance and greater efficiency. Servant leadership emphasizes mutual respect and understanding between all members of a team. This can lead to an increase in trust among team members, which can help build an effective and reliable team.

Servant leadership encourages leaders to seek out different perspectives and ideas to understand the world in a more comprehensive way. This can enhance the way leaders in law enforcement and the military understand the population they serve, enabling them to be better prepared to address issues in a more effective way.

Influencers who are servant leaders foster an environment of collaboration and integration of all teammates in decision-making, thus enabling all members to contribute their ideas and expertise to the team. When there is buy-in, this results in better decision-making and problem-solving capabilities.

In a profession intently focused on outcomes instead of impact, servant leadership enables leaders to focus on continuous improvement. When our cultures provide leaders with room to fail and grow, it encourages leaders to be reflective and open-minded in order to create an environment conducive to the development of better work ethics and quality. This can help improve the overall effectiveness of a law enforcement or military organization.

Virtue-Based Leadership

Virtue-based leadership is a style of leadership in which leaders use the principles of ethics and morality to guide their decisions and provide guidance to their team. It emphasizes the importance of moral values and ethical behavior when making decisions and managing people. Virtue-based leadership emphasizes the importance of moral values and ethical behavior not just as a means to an end but as the foundational principle for leading people and groups.

The primary aim of virtue-based leadership is to create a workplace culture where teammates have a strong sense of values and moral responsibility to themselves, their colleagues, and the organization. Such a culture fosters a commitment to excellence, a spirit of collaboration, and an environment where everybody feels included and respected. In this way, virtue-based leadership helps to create an organization that is dedicated to achieving its core values and objectives.

Virtue-based leadership helps influence people by providing a strong, value-based foundation for the team. It encourages everyone to have a sense of direct responsibility for the organization and helps build strong relationships. It also sets an example of ethical and virtuous behavior and encourages others to follow that example.

Virtue-based leadership helps to ensure that the goals and objectives of the organization are achievable and stay true to moral values. It helps to remind people of the importance of ethical behavior, even if it means sacrificing personal gain in favor of the greater good. This helps create a culture of camaraderie in the workplace and builds trust among colleagues.

For me, I advocate for this modality to help officers overcome challenges. Virtue-based leadership helps to inspire employees by reinforcing the importance of ethical principles. It encourages people to stay true to their values even in difficult situations and fosters an atmosphere in which people feel appreciated and respected. This helps to create long-term commitment and loyalty to the organization and team. Ultimately this helps to create a culture of excellence and foster success in the workplace.

Leadership Development

Developing leaders is the most important role for police executives, and so many fail critically at their primary role. Without healthy and prepared leaders, the agency is grossly unprepared to meet the needs of fluid environments. This leads to failure in the field, which is often accompanied by discipline. It's an endless cycle that creates distrust, high stress, and career unfulfillment.

As it stands today, most leadership development consists of schools and off-site training like the FBI National Academy. These schools are great for reminders, but leadership is a daily practice. Hanging a certificate on our wall doesn't make us leaders, and this distinction has fundamental and long-term consequences.

Police executives have a moral and ethical responsibility to their communities and personnel to develop their teams and leaders.

The best way to develop police leaders is by providing on-the-job training opportunities, continuing education, mentorship from experienced leaders, and opportunities to observe leadership in action. Additionally, agencies may wish to provide leadership development courses or workshops that focus on topics such as problem-solving, conflict resolution, communication, decision-making, and team building. Furthermore, an agency's leadership should be a role model and mentor by emphasizing the importance of professional and ethical conduct. Finally, providing recognition and encouragement will help foster a culture of leadership, as well as reinforce positive behavior and recognize achievement.

The Benefits of Strong Leadership Inside an Agency

Strong leadership inside an agency can bring many positive benefits to the entire organization and its members. A strong leader has the ability to motivate and inspire their team to reach their goals and strive for success while also providing direction and guidance. Good leaders are able to create a positive work environment that is conducive to innovation, growth, and high performance.

Here are some of the top benefits of strong leadership inside an agency:

1. **Builds trust and loyalty.** A strong leader is able to build trust and loyalty among their team members. This trust creates a cohesive team that all feel as though they are part of something bigger. With trust also comes respect and admiration for a leader willing to take on the responsibilities of leading a team.

2. **Increases productivity.** Strong leadership provides direction and guidance, allowing team members to quickly learn their roles and expectations, resulting in increased productivity. When teams feel confident in their leader, it is much easier to stay focused and work together efficiently.

3. **Enhances morale.** A strong leader can create a sense of camaraderie, which helps to keep morale high in the workplace. Having a leader willing to stand behind their team and listen to their ideas gives employees confidence and a feeling of accomplishment in working as a team toward a common goal.

4. **Solidifies relationships.** Leadership creates an interdependent relationship between the leader and team members, and an environment that allows for healthy relationships to be formed. Having a leader able to communicate at different levels in the organization creates a strong foundation of understanding and cooperation.

5. **Raises recruitment and retention.** The current police applicant is more educated and worldly compared to previous generations. Applicants have choices on which agencies to work for and they are asking the right questions to help make a decision. How is the culture here? How is the leadership here? I didn't ask those questions during my hiring process. With more informed prospects, it's only reasonable that the policing profession modifies with them.

Differentiated Communication

The 5 Love Languages is a self-help book written by Dr. Gary Chapman. It theorizes that fundamentally there are five distinct communication styles that people use to express and experience love: **words of affirmation, quality time, receiving gifts, acts of service, and physical touch**. The primary idea is that each individual has a particular love language, and if partners learn each other's language, it will lead to a deeper understanding of each other and improved relationships. The book also contains practical advice on how to communicate love effectively.

I read this book in 2012 after Kristen and I went to therapy together to work on our marriage. We were miscommunicating with one another. Kristen "received love" from me through massages, cuddling, and doing kind gestures for her. I "received love" from her telling me nice things about how I am as a father and husband (words of affirmation). When we wanted to "show love" to each other, we communicated in the ways that we liked to receive love as individuals. Instead of telling Kristen what a good person she is (she is!), she felt loved the most when I lay with her on the couch. Consequently, instead of her buying me a gift, Kristen learned how to affirm me. Together, we learned the right language to communicate—and, most importantly, understand—with one another.

This communication can be applied to leadership roles. Too often I've seen leaders expect their teammates to meet the leader where they're at. My suggestion is for leaders to meet their teammates—all of them—where *they* are at. It will require the leader to embrace discomfort and try new things.

LEADERSHIP CODE OF CONDUCT

1. **POSSESS HIGH CHARACTER.** Great leaders influence their teams by leading by example. A leader who models good behavior and sets a positive example is far more likely to influence the team than not. Having character protects us from leading from a position as "do as I say." Instead, leaders with a high degree of character tell their teams, "Let me show you how." Having high character helps leaders remove and maintain healthy levels of ego. All highly effective leaders have strong mental and moral values.
2. **EXHIBIT HUMILITY.** The fundamental mistake most leaders make is their desire to appear all-knowing. It's impossible for a leader to know everything. This is where a humble leader can acknowledge their shortcomings and even rely on a teammate who may know more than them in a certain area. Humility helps build esprit de corps, and teammates learn that it's more important to "get it right than be right."
3. **DEMONSTRATE PATIENCE.** Teammates are going to learn at different paces. A good leader is patient with

those teammates lagging behind. Patient leaders know that success takes time, and training our teammates requires a steady, consistent hand. Patient leaders also provide a sense of calmness for their teams which is especially critical in high-stress environments.

4. **OWN EVERYTHING.** Great leaders defer credit and own blame. More than that, great leaders own everything. A teammate is underperforming? It's a reflection on the leader. When leaders own everything, including their own faults, it creates an accountable team culture and minimizes excuses. Accountability is a cornerstone of highly successful teams. We all must be accountable to each other and ourselves. Leaders do not cast blame. Rather, we triage problems to a successful resolution.

5. **VALUES/ETHOS.** There are few things more detrimental to esprit de corps than dishonest and untrustworthy leaders. Team members thrive in a culture where they don't question the information they're receiving or the motives of the leader. Our teammates are watching everything we do. As leaders, we must serve others selflessly and honorably. We can only accomplish this by leading virtuously. Leaders and organizations should have core values defined to serve as a guide for decision-making and problem-solving. Values are nonnegotiable, and leaders must never compromise them. The best leaders understand the role ethos plays in team performance.

6. **EMOTIONAL INTELLIGENCE.** EQ is mandatory in effective leadership. A core of EQ is self-awareness. The leader needs to know who they are (strengths and weaknesses) if they are to inspire others successfully. Leaders must develop relationships, which is accomplished by influencing their teammates through model and example. Leaders with high EQ reduce team stress, teams sustain success longer, inspire confidence in their teammates, and, most importantly, are strong communicators. Leaders with

high EQ have smaller egos, which fosters esprit de corps and always ensures the "team" is foremost. The most overlooked aspect of leadership is what I refer to as "self-lead." Self-lead is the ability to manage yourself first. Proper "self-leadership" helps us control our own emotions, reduce personal stress, not be defensive or vindictive, and maintain a positive mindset for the team. Leaders should "respond" to situations rather than "react" emotionally.

7. **COMMUNICATION.** Without a doubt, the most neglected or deficient leadership skill is effective communication. Great leaders all have strong abilities to actively listen and process information quickly and appropriately. Great leaders understand they won't always have an answer, but they engage, listen, and follow up. Effective leaders listen more than they speak. They dig into the details and never miss an opportunity to connect with a teammate. Relationships are the bedrock for organizational success and communication is a prerequisite for effective leadership. Strong leaders tend to be master communicators.

8. **SERVE AUTHENTICALLY.** A leader's job is to influence and inspire the team. If we're not genuine people, we will not be able to influence others. Being authentic enables the team to see each other "as is," not "what I want you to see." This allows people to form deeper relationships and develop a "buy-in" approach. Being authentic forms strong teams, and in service professions, serving authentically is critical to forming transcendent relationships with the community.

9. **GOALS AND EXPECTATIONS.** Just like children, our teammates operate well in a structured environment with clear goals and expectations. Teams should have collective goals that drive performance. In that, though, every teammate should have personal goals for their careers/lives. What is commonly lost is the leader's active involvement in helping their teammates accomplish their goals. Leaders

must take ownership of their teammates and help them chart a path to success.

10. **TEAMWORK/RELATIONSHIPS.** Great leaders first extend trust to the team. Only when we give it will our teammates reciprocate. Far too often I've heard leaders tell their teams, "You need to earn my trust." What are we telling them? You must trust me first and hopefully I learn to trust you back? No. We trust our teammates and set a good example. We have faith that they will reward our trust and focus on them. This is how relationships become **relational** and not transactional.

Trauma-Informed Leadership

Trauma-informed leadership is a leadership approach whereby leaders acknowledge and understand the impact of trauma on individuals, groups, and organizations and proactively create a supportive, emotionally safe, and mindful environment. It goes beyond providing mental health services by establishing a trauma-informed organizational culture that minimizes negative outcomes and provides healing opportunities to those affected. This approach acknowledges the complex realities of trauma and builds resilience and empowers those affected by it. Trauma-informed leadership promotes the safety, respect, well-being, and dignity of all people by focusing on understanding the impact of trauma on an individual's life. It involves recognizing the importance of addressing a person's experiences, beliefs, and values while creating a work environment where stressors that could cause further trauma are minimized. It also involves the implementation of policies and procedures that are designed to promote safety and prevent additional trauma.

Strong leadership inside an agency can be a huge benefit to the entire organization. Leaders are essential in creating the positive work environment needed to encourage the growth and success of the entire agency. By creating a professional and positive environment, strong leadership can help to bring out the best in each and every team member.

Ask yourself the following questions:

1. What leadership changes can you make today for your teams?
2. What would your squad/platoon/department look like with more effective leadership?
3. What can we do to better support the leaders who are influencing in effective ways?

CHAPTER VII

CULTURE

"TRUE BELONGING IS THE SPIRITUAL PRACTICE OF BELIEVING IN AND BELONGING TO YOURSELF SO DEEPLY THAT YOU CAN SHARE YOUR MOST AUTHENTIC SELF WITH THE WORLD AND FIND SACREDNESS IN BOTH BEING A PART OF SOMETHING AND STANDING ALONE IN THE WILDERNESS. TRUE BELONGING DOES NOT REQUIRE YOU TO CHANGE WHO YOU ARE; IT REQUIRES YOU TO BE WHO YOU ARE."
-BRENÉ BROWN

Cultures

When we think of the word culture, we don't typically think of everything that goes into strong cultures. I got my first job at McDonald's when I was 14. I remember the pride I felt wearing that polo shirt with the Golden Arches. I recall clocking in, filling a role, and serving as best I knew how. At 14, my perspective was naturally minimal. Do you know what got me to apply for the job? I got the job because my friend Brian also worked there, and he said to me, "Come work at McDonald's, you'll love it there. They give you a five-dollar credit for lunch on every shift." I was hooked! It doesn't take a lot to impress a young teenager at their first job.

Unfortunately, workplace cultures in the adult world need more than a lunch credit to keep team members around. Many young job prospects now search for a career where they can have an impact and feel rewarded. Much of the 20th century in America was about survival and how to become prosperous; being able to provide for your family was the primary concern. As Maslow's Hierarchy of Needs illustrates, safety and security were primary concerns.

Police culture is often seen as being toxic, with a reputation for being unresponsive to criticism, biased toward certain groups, and prone to excessive violence. There are many reasons for this, some of which are due to institutionalized structures, systemic inequities, and others stemming from individual officers' attitudes.

Police culture is often characterized by a "code of silence," whereby officers are encouraged not to speak out against one another, even if it means that bad behavior will continue. This code of silence not only prevents natural consequences from occurring but it can also create a culture of denial and secrecy. This silencing of dissent can lead to an environment of abuse and misconduct, both of which can be incredibly toxic.

Some inner-city communities even view police as some form of occupying force in some communities, as they are perceived to be oppressive toward and biased against certain racial, ethnic, and socioeconomic groups. These views from some communities may be based on a perverse perspective, and that's why transparency is so critical. If communities don't feel that the police department is being held accountable for their performance, trust can further cultivate an environment of fear and mistrust between the public and police and can lead to unequal and often violent interactions between the two groups.

Police culture is also often excessively competitive. Within a militarized police system, law enforcement often favors an aggressive approach to dealing with crime; they are often rewarded if they "win" against criminals and punished if they do not. This amplifies the violence of police work and encourages officers to prioritize aggression.

At its core, police culture is often defined by an aggressive response to crime and an obsessive competition with suspects. When combined with the code of silence and pervasive mistrust of minorities and the poor, this leads to harsh consequences and a toxic environment. In order to move away from this culture, police forces must focus on accountability, transparency, and trust-building with the public more than ever before.

In police cultures, we've become conditioned to go along to get along. The meaningful relationships we require for connection and belonging? We now use that energy on relationships that can help us survive. You see, we went from value-driven relationships (relational) to safety-focused relationships (transactional). Have you ever known two coworkers to be best friends for one year and enemies the next? When two people come together with a common goal, great synergy can happen, even if it's for a short time. When two people come together with the same values, that's when long-lasting and meaningful relationships can develop. This takes a lot of practice to master. I don't think we'll ever get there without being annoyingly cynical or blissfully utopian.

Building resilient organizational cultures requires a daily commitment. Human connection and meaningful relationships are the easiest and most cost-efficient way to achieve this. What holds so many organizations back from consuming the necessary energy to forge strong relationships? Effort and understanding. When we form deep bonds with just one person, it fosters a deeper trust in the world. Have you ever seen a friend after they have their first serious relationship? They changed. They're more confident. Have you wondered why? They had a meaningful connection that transcended them.

Improving police culture is a key goal of many law enforcement organizations. As the public's trust in the police decreases, police forces must work to ensure that the culture of their departments reflects the best of community-oriented policing. With that said, it is important to recognize that improving police culture is far from an easy task. It requires significant changes in the way police interact with communities and how police officers think about their responsibilities and the service they provide to the public. The following chapter will detail some of the most practical ways to improve police culture and help foster a more positive relationship between law enforcement agencies and the public.

What's Your Code?

Values and morality are essential components of a fulfilling life of service. They provide the framework for how we interact with the world around us and how we can best contribute to the greater good. Values and morality are the foundation of our beliefs and actions, and they help us to make decisions that are in line with our highest intentions.

Values are the guiding principles that shape our beliefs and actions. They are the standards by which we measure our behavior and determine the right and wrong of our actions. Values provide us with a sense of purpose and direction in life. They give us a sense of direction and help us to make decisions that are in line with our highest values.

Morality is the set of rules and standards that govern our behavior. It is the basis of our ethical conduct and guides us in making decisions that are in line with our values. Morality helps us to be mindful of our actions and to act in a way that is consistent with our highest principles.

When we live our lives in accordance with our values and morality, we are able to make decisions that are in line with our highest intentions and that lead to a more fulfilling life of service. We are more likely to act in ways that benefit others and that contribute to the greater good. We are able to make decisions that are in line with our values and that help us to live a life of purpose and meaning.

Living a life of service requires us to be mindful of our values and morality. We must strive to be aware of our actions and to act in a way that is consistent with our highest principles. We must strive to make decisions that are in line with our values and that lead to a more fulfilling life of service. With a strong foundation of values and morality, we can lead a life of service that is meaningful and rewarding.

The Nonnegotiables

The importance of virtue and values in leadership roles cannot be underestimated. To become highly effective leaders, we must be quality humans first. Effective leaders must possess traits such as integrity, trustworthiness, bravery, and self-discipline in order to gain respect, admiration, and loyalty from those who have elected or appointed them. With these traits, leaders are able to guide their teams through difficult times and inspire others to reach new heights.

Having virtue and values allows leaders to inspire their teams, make difficult decisions in times of crisis, and act as a moral compass for their teams. By embodying moral standards, leaders can serve as an example not only for their organization but for the larger society. Virtue and values enable leaders to be respected, trusted and admired in the eyes of their employees and colleagues.

Similarly, having virtue and values within an organization enables leaders to form a set of shared values and beliefs amongst their teams. Leaders who foster a strong sense of camaraderie, empathy, and loyalty amongst their employees are better suited to drive a successful organization. These values and beliefs form the basis for successful decision-making and ensure that the team is united against a common goal or problem.

Finally, the importance of virtue and values in leadership roles lies in their ability to define a leader's public image. A leader who is seen as trustworthy, honest, and unafraid to take action in times of crisis is one who can inspire those around them to do the same. Through virtue and values, leadership can be a positive influence in our communities and cultures, one that can inspire others and make a difference in the world.

Virtue and values are essential elements of effective leadership. They provide leaders with an ethical and moral compass, help to create a culture of shared values and beliefs within the organization, and can add tremendous weight to a leader's public image. Without these elements, leaders may be in the dark when deciding what course of action to take or may find it difficult to attract the respect of those they lead. Thus, it is important that leaders strive to embody virtue and values in order to effectively lead their teams.

Foster Respect, Empathy, & Vulnerability

One of the most effective ways to improve police culture is to foster respect and empathy inside the agency and within the community. Empathy is a major culture driver, and it must come from the chief executive. Too often, elected bodies are not using empathy or other emotional intelligence (EQ) markers to make hiring decisions on chiefs. Sadly, we continue to repeat the problem hire after hire. We're largely hiring the wrong type of leader for the role of chief executive. Empathy must be the first factor considered. I worked for a chief with little empathy, and it was a nightmare. He legitimately appeared to take pleasure in the demise of others.

In order to do this, police departments must ensure that their training and hiring processes take into account factors such as the backgrounds and culture of prospective officers. When officers are trained with a human-centric approach and learn to respect people from different backgrounds, the likelihood increases that they will treat others with respect in the field. Additionally, police should emphasize the importance of identifying and addressing bias in their interactions with the public. Police officers must strive to be impartial and nonjudgmental as much as possible, and training courses should heavily emphasize the importance of treating communities and individuals with respect.

Communication

Police agencies have become silos of information and personnel. Many agencies have multiple closed schedules and track vacation time in private methods. Additionally, many agencies do not communicate effectively and, worse, intentionally withhold critical information from teammates. This leads to distrust and unhealthy cultures. Communication is a two-way street, and to work effectively, all parties must communicate truthfully, openly, and respectfully. We forget that behind the badges are humans dealing with a variety of issues at work and at home. Many are carrying shame and not the healthiest versions of themselves. We must resist making assumptions about each other. By communicating and connecting regularly with one another, we work to fill in missing gaps of information, which inevitably helps us find inner peace.

This same approach should be applied to the community. As cops, we pride ourselves on knowing when we're being lied to. We're conditioned to call out liars and disliked for it. What happens when we don't fully disclose unprotected information or speak from a place of arrogance? The same thing—they'll dislike us! As police and community leaders, we should always model the example of what we want. If we want truth and excellence, we first give truth and excellence. This will help police officers be more effective at reaching more citizens where they're at by forging unique and positive relationships with citizens. This could involve anything from attending community events to meeting with local representatives to discuss policing issues.

Leaders could do a better job at motivating and incentivizing officers to develop unique solutions to reach the community. Sadly, many good officers report being stonewalled with such ideas. Why and where do these rejections and refusal to adapt come from? We will work to answer every single question being asked because it's *that* important for the future of American public safety.

Lastly, police departments should also create and promote ways in which the public can give feedback and provide constructive criticism of their service. This could be through social media, public forums, or citizen review boards. This way, members of the public can give honest opinions and be heard in an effective and safe way. Police officers could benefit from developing a more resilient mindset to weather any criticism that comes in. Criticism should be welcomed as a way to improve. I wanted to be the best police officer I could be. To do that, I needed and welcomed criticism. Sometimes it was hard to hear, and it still is. But, once the sting wears off, we must push through the emotions and make a reasonable, logical, and healthy decision. Emotions always fade, and sometimes our emotional decisions last a lifetime.

Affirmations & Compliments

Affirmations in the workplace have powerful effects on teammates' confidence and morale. **Affirmations** often take the form of verbal statements and gestures of recognition given by colleagues and supervisors for good work, such as giving compliments or expressing appreciation, recognizing achievements and successes, or motivating employees to strive for the next goal.

It can also involve providing feedback on how employees can improve their work performance.

A **compliment** is given to someone to express admiration or approval for something they have done. An affirmation is given to someone to reinforce positive thinking. Many leaders in policing struggle to affirm their officers consistently. Without reinforcement, officers don't fully understand their performance track. Affirmations and other feedback help us to make adjustments and corrections to our behaviors. Without critical feedback from peers and leaders, many officers have difficulty advancing their careers. If we want to retain top talent, we must affirm them more. Affirmations go a long way to help officers feel respected and valued at their agency.

Ensure Fair Investigations and Disciplinary Actions

It is essential that police executives treat all team members equally and fairly in investigations and disciplinary actions. Police executives or their designees must investigate internal matters fairly and promptly in order to maintain the integrity and trustworthiness of the agency and to protect the safety of the public. Fair and prompt investigations can prevent and discourage officers from engaging in misconduct or other illegal activities.

Additionally, investigating complaints quickly will help to reduce any stress or trauma that may have occurred, allowing the matter to be resolved quickly and efficiently. Doing so will also help to create a culture of accountability and transparency within the department, which can improve public trust and help foster a cooperative law enforcement relationship with the community. When officers feel safe and trusted within their agency, they're more likely to be open and engaging with the community.

Police chiefs should never target their officers. This type of action can lead to a hostile working environment and could result in unfair treatment of officers. Instead, police chiefs should focus on the performance and accountability of the officers, ensuring they are equipped to best serve their communities. A coaching and mentor program within the agency could help fill the void where traditional leadership is lacking within the agency.

In my final two weeks at the police department, one of the sergeants played a fun prank on me. A citizen found a small statue of Santa Muerte, the Mexican patron saint, and placed it on my desk. In the drug subculture, Santa Muerte has a meaning of death, and drug traffickers have been known to use Santa Muerte as a form of good luck. Santa Muerte by herself is not controversial. The sergeant put the Santa Muerte statue on my desk and told me it was to ward off evil spirits during my final two weeks and keep me safe.

I tried to strap Santa Muerte into my passenger seat so she could come on patrol with me and keep me safe. But she wouldn't fit neatly in my patrol car and had to stay back at the station, so I put her by the back door. After my shift ended, I went home and forgot about the statue. You would have thought I robbed a bank.

I was woken by numerous calls and text messages. Without being fair or impartial, making it totally personal, Chief Pathe told me I was under investigation. I panicked and asked for what, and he advised me of the statue. Here is where I suffered a moral injury: when Chief Pathe explained to me that he had concerns about officer safety because the statue was used for "evil purposes." I began to laugh, fully recognizing the misunderstanding. As I explained what happened, I assumed it would have been met with, "Ah, I understand now. Thanks for explaining." Instead, I was again told that I was under investigation.

I was standing in my foyer and began to experience a panic attack. I fell to the ground, believing I was dying; that's how bad it was. I remember telling Kristen, "I'm never going to get away from this man. He won't leave me alone." Kristen rubbed my back and reminded me I was leaving there.

Several days later the investigation was complete and I was now in my final week. Chief Pathe informed me, "You are being disciplined, and a letter will be filed on Guardian (our online tracking system)." I never received that letter, and it was another bullying tactic aimed at causing me stress. Mission accomplished!

A week later I rode off into the moonlight, head low, ashamed of how my career ended. I even heard they got me a shadow box with all my badges in it. To this day, I never received it. They canceled two separate events that were scheduled to celebrate my career and never rescheduled.

When executives wield their "power" with a sword instead of a pen, trust cannot be established.

Establish Clear Goals; Set Expectations and Values

Make sure everyone in the organization understands and is aligned with the organization's mission and values. This will help create a common understanding and basis for all decisions. Develop a system for resolving conflicts and issues in a collaborative way. This sets healthy expectations and guidelines for how to successfully navigate the next conflict.

Setting proper expectations is an important leadership skill because it helps to ensure that teams have a shared understanding of the tasks they must complete, the goals they must meet, and the timelines and resources that will be used. It helps to build a sense of trust and sets the stage for successful execution and achievement of objectives. Proper expectations also can help to prevent miscommunication, build trust and reliability, improve morale, and increase productivity, creativity, and collaboration.

Invest in Leadership Development

Ensure leadership teams have the skills necessary to foster a positive environment that aligns with the mission and values of the organization. Leadership development is key to creating a healthy organizational culture. Successful leaders ensure everyone is given a chance to give input and make decisions that can improve the organization. Leaders should always provide opportunities for team members to learn and grow.

Here are the top eight ways to develop into a better leader:

1. **Mentorship.** Allowing current leaders to pair up with less experienced officers is an effective way to recognize the value of experience while giving others a chance to grow. When officers are mentored by senior leaders outside of their chain of command, it provides unique opportunities to grow.
2. **Model proper behavior.** Leaders should act as role models and demonstrate integrity, honesty, and respectfulness.
3. **Instill confidence.** Offer frequent, constructive feedback and praise that reinforces positive behaviors.
4. **Train and develop.** Sponsor training programs to teach skills related to leadership, communication, problem-solving, and crisis management.
5. **Create an environment conducive to growth.** Foster relationships between senior and junior employees and promote collaboration across all levels of the organization.
6. **Encourage self-reflection.** Provide space and time for team members to reflect on their progress and how to improve. When officers focus on their errors and mistakes, it provides an opportunity to improve. When leaders collaborate with their teams on failures, junior officers can learn from more experienced officers. Instead of feeling shame, officers learn and grow. Ask for their input on where they'd like to go and how to get there.
7. **Support professional development.** Promote and fund activities such as certification programs and continuing education classes to help employees gain skills.
8. **Affirmations.** Showcase team members' accomplishments to the rest of the organization and reward them for their hard work.

Provide Training on Emotional Intelligence

Developing emotional intelligence among employees is important for creating strong relationships and trust in the organization, which supports a healthy organizational culture. The benefit of police officers attending emotional intelligence training is that it helps increase their skills in regulating their own emotions and managing any emotions that may arise in stressful or particularly emotional situations. This can help with more effective communication and decision-making in their line of work, as well as promote empathy and a better understanding of those they are interacting with. This can lead to better outcomes, greater safety for officers and the public, and stronger community-police relations.

Hold Leaders Accountable

Establish clear expectations around how leaders should treat employees and set consequences when they fail to do so. This will help ensure ethical standards are met and held to. It is important for organizational culture for police executives to hold sergeants and other junior leaders accountable in order to create a strong culture focused on integrity and accountability. It sets a standard that all officers and staff associated with the organization should abide by and reinforces that conduct unbecoming of a law enforcement officer is not tolerated. Officers that are held accountable feel more respected and motivated to act in accordance with the organization's values. Additionally, it reinforces the rule of law and ensures that the public has faith in the department.

Provide Recognition

Develop a recognition program that acknowledges and rewards team members for their hard work and contributions. Recognize and reward outstanding team members and accomplishments. This will show how much the organization values its employees. When we recognize our team members—*all* members—we create a welcoming culture for people to feel valued and appreciated. This undoubtedly curbs the retention issues plaguing policing today.

Foster Wellness

Create a culture that respects all employees and provides resources, such as confidential and nonpunitive mental and emotional health solutions. Leaders have tremendous influence over organizational wellness. Promote an attitude of creativity and collaboration rather than fear and competition.

Improving police culture is a key goal of many law enforcement organizations. To effectively improve police culture, it is important to foster respect and empathy, open up lines of communication between law enforcement and the community, and ensure that all investigations and disciplinary actions are fair and impartial. By working to address these issues, police officers can help create a culture of trust and accountability between the police and the public.

How does that happen? Lack of courage and a healthy mind. I think the mental and emotional health crisis in this country has paralyzed so many leaders from making courageous and necessary decisions. Instead, we choose the path of least resistance. We'll let unhealthy leaders continue to create toxic cultures and take hostages.

CHAPTER VIII

WELLNESS

"WHAT LIES BEHIND YOU AND WHAT LIES IN FRONT OF YOU, PALES IN COMPARISON TO WHAT LIES INSIDE OF YOU."
-RALPH WALDO EMERSON

More than any other chapter in this book, this one is the most important. That's why this chapter completes Act II. It is where it all changed for me and hopefully you too. There wasn't one particular thing that awakened in me, but I do remember the moment I stopped "hoping" and "wishing" and decided to start DOING. It all had to do with me, myself, and I. That's the point of this important chapter—wellness starts and ends with ourselves. Self-care and stress management are no one else's responsibility but our own. Now imagine a police agency that also prioritizes officer wellness. The officer feels supported at home and at work. It's the goal of why I'm doing this movement.

Wellness is misunderstood by many executives, and the profession is slow to understand just how critical wellness is. I was beating the drum on this years ago; the current way we nurture officers is unsustainable. Eventually, cops will stop showing up because of how we treat them as a profession. That is what's happening right now. Cop prospects aren't showing up like they used to because of the danger of the job and how we treat each other inside the profession. It all starts and ends with wellness.

When we're not well, we're not the best versions of ourselves. When leaders are unwell, they could affect the entire team. I came from an agency of about thirty police officers. Most were married with children. Our chief wasn't leading thirty officers; he was leading over 100 people because our spouses and children were on this ride with us. When every spouse in the agency has disdain for the chief, we ought to be asking questions about that. If we truly want to take care of police officers and their families, we must start with who was selected to lead our police agencies. Nothing ruins a police agency more than the wrong chief hire.

What is Wellness?

Wellness, as it pertains to policing, involves the creation of an environment and culture that values and supports the physical, mental, emotional, and spiritual health of all officers. This involves providing officers with the necessary resources to deal with the daily stresses of the job, addressing unhealthy practices such as macho behavior and extreme militarization, and creating a supportive culture that values self-care, compassion, and community. Ultimately, it is about creating an organizational culture of health and safety, allowing officers to continue to serve their communities honorably and effectively. When we have healthy agencies, our officers are more likely to stay in the fight. Isn't that the goal?

Dog-Eat-Dog Culture

When police officers have their badges pinned on their chests, they are beaming with pride. I remember the night Kristen was there with me along with my immediate family, grandparents, and in-laws. I had a big smile; nothing could faze me. Little did I know that I was embarking on a career that is *guaranteed* to change you. Few leaders were talking about it when I started in 2008. I came home from Iraq three years earlier thinking I was the definition of resilience. My ignorance, combined with my arrogance, would cause problems for me. Like most of us, when we're not aware of the imminent problem, we tend to be blindsided when we shouldn't have been. We are our worst enemy. I hope you read this book and get out of your own way.

A police officer's mental health can drastically change over time due to the stressors they face daily. Police officers are exposed to a variety of highly stressful incidents and situations that can lead to mental health issues such as post-traumatic stress disorder, depression, and anxiety. These issues can manifest in a variety of ways and can have a long-term negative effect on an officer's mental wellness.

When first joining the police force, officers begin with a strong sense of resilience, determination, and hope. These positive emotions can be bolstered with a strong support system of family and friends. They may also find strength in the sense of community they find in their department and the camaraderie they share in the work they do.

However, as an officer ages on the job, these positive feelings can wear away due to exposure to critical and traumatic incidents. Police officers are often under intense pressure and scrutiny from their superiors, the media, and the public. This can lead to feelings of isolation and loneliness, which can further compound their already existing stress from daily work.

Officers may also experience guilt and self-doubt due to the nature of the work they do. Being exposed to the death of a fellow officer or the trauma of a civilian can cause guilt and feelings of failure. Officers may begin to question the morality of their job and whether it is really making a difference. This can lead to an erosion of self-esteem and an overall feeling of cynicism.

As years go by, officers may also struggle with chronic mental health issues as a result of their daily work. Traumatic experiences can lead to the development of post-traumatic stress disorder, depression, and anxiety disorders. Unaddressed mental health issues can further impact the officer's work and relationships.

For police officers looking to maintain good mental health, some suggestions may include regular exercise, talking to friends and family, and finding a hobby to engage in outside of work. It is important for police officers to take measures to manage their mental health over time and understand that it is completely normal to experience feelings of stress and anxiety. Seeking professional help if needed can also be a helpful step in managing mental health.

How Does Trauma Affect the Brain?

Auditory exclusion is a phenomenon experienced by individuals in a highly intense environment when their focus becomes so intense that all other sounds and sights become blocked out. This is often seen in situations like combat, where the person is so focused on the task at hand and the details of the present moment that they become unaware of all other sounds and sights, making them oblivious to any actual danger or other external stimuli.

Memory gaps can occur in situations of auditory exclusion due to both environmental and psychological reasons. In a stressful or traumatic situation, the individual may remember important parts of the event but have difficulty recalling finer details due to a natural shutting down of memory processing. Additionally, the vividness of the experience could cause certain memories to be enhanced while others are altogether forgotten.

Visual distortion is another phenomenon often seen among those experiencing auditory exclusion. Visual distortion can manifest in a number of ways, from blurred vision and tunnel vision to color shifts and the perception of different shapes and sizes. Visual distortion can be attributed to both the stress of the situation and a heightened neurological response caused by intense focus.

I've experienced all of these phenomena during my years of service. That's why I know they're important to talk about because they affect our thoughts and actions, which in turn develop into behaviors. Knowing is empowering, and as I learned things, I recognized how deficient we are in the profession of alerting cops to potential risks. At the end of the day, reducing our personal harm should be looked at on a sliding scale and not all or nothing. If an officer is managing their mental and emotional health better today than yesterday, let's celebrate and affirm the harm reduction and not ostracize him or her for the manner in which they achieved it.

Stress Management

It is every officer's job to manage their stress. Organization culture and agency leadership also have a direct effect on officer stress; however, individuals must prepare themselves to be the sole determiner of their stress management plan. Stress can be good for us, and we don't talk enough about the different types of stress—distress and eustress.

Distress and **eustress** are two distinct states of the body and mind that can be experienced in response to various internal and external stimuli. Stress is an emotional and physical response to a perceived or real threat, while eustress is a positive form of stress that can help enhance a person's performance and increase motivation.

Stress is usually associated with negative effects such as anxiety, depression, and physical illness. It depletes energy, decreases concentration, and can interfere with daily functioning in severe cases. Additionally, chronic stress has been linked to a number of health problems, such as cardiovascular disease, hypertension, and compromised immunity.

Eustress, on the other hand, is a form of constructive stress that generally has a positive outcome. It is the feeling of excitement and anticipation associated with meeting a challenge or achieving a goal. It can lead to improved performance and creativity and can even help build resilience in certain situations. I refer to this as the "flow state" when I'm locked in on what I'm doing. This is a positive state for humans, especially police officers.

The main differences between stress and eustress are their effect on the body. Whereas stress puts the body in a state of physical tension and arousal, eustress leads to an invigorating response, often with improved performance and greater focus. Additionally, stress is often associated with negative emotions such as fear, anxiety, and anger, whereas eustress is associated with positive emotions such as joy, enthusiasm, and excitement.

Coping Strategies

Adaptive coping strategies are techniques, behaviors, or thoughts that help a person manage stress or difficult situations in a healthy manner. They are usually proactive and positive and can help to problem-solve while still maintaining emotional well-being. Examples of adaptive coping strategies include seeking help from counselors/therapists, talking to friends and family, exercising, relaxation techniques, and making positive lifestyle changes.

Maladaptive coping strategies are ways of managing stress and difficult situations that are often destructive and unhelpful in the long run. Examples of maladaptive coping strategies include excessive substance use, avoidance, isolating oneself, and even violence. These coping mechanisms can lead to further emotional distress or even harm.

After the demotion, I was incapable of managing my stress in healthy ways and used unhealthy and dangerous coping strategies like drugs and alcohol to make myself feel better. I was desperate to stop the pain I was feeling. The shame weighed me down to the point that I was seeking drugs and alcohol to balance myself out. I was emotionally tied to unhealthy substances just to feel "normal." Once I learned about the different coping strategies, it helped me develop a path toward **full-spectrum wellness.**

SOLUTIONS

1. **Physical exercise.** Exercise can help reduce stress, improve mood, and help keep officers physically fit. Our stress and well-being are tied to our physical health. I retired from policing in March 2021, weighing 206 pounds. Two years later, with moderate exercise and mindfulness on wellness, I was down to 177 pounds. The harsh reality for police departments to understand is that repeated and unhealthy levels of stress harm us tremendously. By removing much of the stress in my life, I lost nearly thirty pounds. Physical exercise only may not be enough for some people, though. For me, working out is extremely beneficial, but I need to also develop my brain at the same time. For many police officers, I think they make a critical oversight here. If we are working out every day and not feeling fulfilled, joyful, and confident, we may need additional support, and that's OK!

2. **Get adequate rest.** Sleep is essential for physical and mental health. Getting enough sleep allows officers to be better prepared for the demands of their job. I was not sleeping well my last two years and focused on finding ways

to recover healthier. Lack of quality sleep is a major life disruptor, and we will not become out best versions unless we're getting seven or eight hours of uninterrupted sleep a night. Sleep is a superpower. Like anything else related to our health, we should be constantly evaluating and adjusting. Nothing stays the same forever, so we ought to be mindful of changes occurring and be willing to adjust.

3. **Eat healthy.** Eating a balanced diet helps keep the immune system strong and bodies fueled for the day. Eating nutritiously can also help maintain lower stress levels. I recall all the unhealthy meals we ate at the police department: twelve-inch-long cheesesteaks with a side of large fries and a bottle of soda. Many cops eat unhealthy and that has a direct effect on our physical health, which feeds into our emotional health. Fit police officers are more confident, and that's good for the community and their partners. I've had periods in my life when I was superbly healthy and training. I was eating well and in great shape. I've also had periods where my mental and emotional health was critical and I ate horribly and drank alcohol every day to self-medicate. There is a stark difference in our mental, physical, and emotional health when we eat healthily compared to when we eat poorly. Some of the worst eating habits I had were from when I was an active-duty police officer. Culturally, we were an unhealthy agency.

4. **Reach out for help/embrace vulnerability.** Police officers should have access to mental health services and other assistance programs to help them deal with the challenges of their job and other issues. When I needed help, I made two minor attempts to notify my chain of command. I was embarrassed and carrying shame. I mustered up whatever courage I had and said to my chief, "I'm really struggling..." and he turned it into a conversation about himself. Needing help, I called the behavioral health number on the back of my medical card and got a list of all the providers in my

area. Most police officer benefits are great; mental health therapy is covered by insurance, generally unlimited visits, low co-pays, and all confidential. Therapy carries a stigma with it, and I think that's the biggest crime done to our officers. At one point after I left policing, I had four therapists who all provided me with different and important solutions to help me heal and recover. Science has evolved, and it's a shame that so many cops suffer in silence because their agency doesn't promote therapy.

5. **Practice mindfulness/meditation.** Taking a few moments of quiet time each day for meditation or mindfulness can help officers relax and become better emotionally equipped to handle stressful situations. In 2017, I attended a police training and learned about "guided breathing." I was stressed and anxious at the time and found the breathing exercises to benefit me greatly. Six years later, I implemented breathing exercises into my daily regimen. The convenience of breathing exercises is police officers can do them anywhere.

6. **Take breaks.** Taking breaks or vacation days can help officers recharge and get a sense of perspective. Police agencies are missing tremendous opportunities to enrich their officers by not acknowledging mental health and wellness. Imagine a police executive who promotes "wellness days" where cops can take off to recover from the stresses of the job. I've seen chiefs vilify officers for taking "mental health days," and it's some of the saddest mistreatment of police officers I've seen.

7. **Be proactive!** Leaders and officers should watch out more closely for themselves and others. Officers should monitor their own thoughts, feelings, and behaviors and take time to recognize their own feelings of anger, grief, or stress. Human connection goes a long way to not having officers slip through the cracks. There are three levels of care: 1) self-care, 2) buddy care, and 3) leader care. If the individual

officer is not taking care of themselves, then their buddy should step in and say something. If that isn't happening, then their leader should be the last resort. So many leaders are not investing in their officers because they're also unhealthy. There are three levels of awareness to prevent officer suicide, and we are drastically failing because, as a profession, we are grossly unwell.

8. **Establish a support system!** Building strong relationships with supportive coworkers and families can help officers lean on each other when needed. More than anything on this list, having a strong peer support program can really help officers on the daily and work to keep them from missing time at work. Peer support and human connection save lives!

Peer Support

Peer support for police is a type of support that involves officers helping and supporting each other in times of difficulty. This type of support could involve anything from providing emotional support to aiding in the day-to-day operations of an officer's life and work. This type of support is important as it provides officers with an outlet to discuss their feelings or concerns with someone they can trust or who understands their situation. Peer support can help reduce stress, anxiety, and fatigue and can also be used to help officers deal with traumatic incidents or difficult times in their life. It can also provide a safe environment where officers can discuss incidents they have experienced and gain knowledge from their peers. When we support our officers, we can expect them to build resilience, which helps to protect them in future incidents as well where trauma is present.

Here are other benefits of having a peer support program:

1. **Increased morale/resilience.** Research suggests that peer support programs can help police officers increase their morale and engagement in their police work. Through such programs, officers have an opportunity to discuss

and share concerns and ask for help and support. Officers have been shown to be more resilient when they heal and recover from a traumatic incident.

2. **Higher performance.** Police officers can often perform better when surrounded by peers who understand their job and related stressors. Peer support programs can provide a sense of camaraderie and support among officers, helping to increase their productivity.
3. **Improved adaptability.** Officers who participate in peer support programs can benefit from a greater ability to cope with change and remain adaptable in their police work. Such programs can also help officers adopt new strategies quickly and more effectively.
4. **Mental health advocacy.** By allowing officers to discuss and share their experiences, peer support programs can provide essential psychological support. This can help reduce stress and mental health issues such as PTSD.
5. **Increased awareness.** Participating in peer support programs can give officers access to a wealth of knowledge and advice from their fellow officers. This can help them improve their decision-making and leadership skills.

Cognitive Behavioral Therapy

Cognitive behavioral therapy (CBT) is a psychological treatment modality that has been used to help police officers with various difficulties. It helps police officers identify and modify cognitive distortions and behavioral maladaptive responses that they may experience in their work. CBT focuses on helping officers recognize the links between their thoughts, feelings, and behaviors. Thus, it can help to change the thought patterns that trigger negative emotions and behaviors in response to the stressful circumstances of police work.

CBT for police officers can help them to develop healthier ways of thinking in order to cope better with the stress and potential danger of their job. It also helps officers to identify, clarify, and modify inaccurate beliefs about themselves and their work. This can help lower their overall levels of stress, increase their sense of competence and self-efficacy, and help them to remain focused on their tasks. Wouldn't less stress in your life be awesome!?

Through CBT, police officers can learn how to manage their emotions more effectively. This includes developing better coping and communication strategies. This can help reduce the likelihood of officers responding aggressively in challenging situations and reduce their risk of post-traumatic stress disorder.

I'll say this with absolute conviction: CBT saved my life, and it can yours, too. CBT can help you to remain mentally and emotionally healthy in the face of the highly stressful and often dangerous work that you do. Don't you want to stay in the fight?

- **Increased self-awareness.** CBT helps individuals to become more aware of their thoughts, feelings, and behaviors. By recognizing how these three components are interrelated, people can gain insight into why they behave a certain way and how to make positive changes.

- **Improved relationships.** CBT can help individuals improve their relationships by teaching them how to express their thoughts and feelings more effectively and how to build healthier relationships with others.

- **Stress management.** CBT can help individuals manage stress more effectively by teaching them problem-solving skills, relaxation techniques, and positive ways of thinking.

- **Improved self-esteem.** By identifying and challenging negative thought patterns, CBT helps individuals create more positive self-images.

- **Coping strategies.** For individuals who have experienced traumatic events, CBT can help them to process the event, reduce distress related to it, and create a healthier sense of self.

Think about your mental and emotional state right now. Where are you deficient, and what are you doing well? Look at the above list. Could you benefit from therapy? I've been in therapy for years and it has changed my life immensely. As police officers, we are some of the most stubborn groups of people, and because of that, we struggle to overcome our challenges. Resilience requires accountability. We can't be afraid to grow and heal. Maybe, just maybe, you'll finally start to love the reflection in the mirror. I guarantee your fears and worries about therapy are much worse than reality. Sit down with a professional you respect, share parts of your life in a safe space, and learn about yourself. Maybe, just maybe, your anxiety will be reduced. What do you have to fear? I promise the worse thing that will happen to you is you heal and improve your life. Be careful—it's dangerous!

EMDR (Eye Movement Desensitization and Reprocessing)

EMDR (eye movement desensitization and reprocessing) is a form of therapy designed to treat mental health trauma. It helps to break the bonds of traumatic memories and use more adaptive responses to the triggers and stress of these memories. During EMDR, the therapist guides the patient through specific sets of eye movements and other tactile activities. By constantly changing the focus of the patient's thinking throughout the therapy session, the patient is able to slowly and effectively process traumatic memories and stimuli. This encourages the patient to think of the trauma and its associated feelings as "past events" that can be better dealt with and understood as opposed to reliving them again and again.

Because of the structure of EMDR, it is especially effective for first responders and veterans who have experienced high levels of trauma in the line of duty. Unlike traditional therapy, the eye movement techniques and activities used in EMDR help these individuals to stay connected and engaged in the therapeutic process while still being able to process their memories and trauma in a safe and controlled environment. For individuals who have experienced severe trauma, EMDR can be an essential component in their journey to recovery.

When I separated from the police department in 2021, I had a lot of work to do on myself. I began going through EMDR treatment, and it had a profound effect on my emotional state. As someone highly sensitive and carrying some big insecurities, I knew I had to attack my emotional flaws in order to build my resilience. I wanted to be able to talk about everything painful that ever happened to me and be able to communicate those experiences. EMDR helped me to view my history from a third-party perspective. It helped to remove the emotional torment of my memories and organize them in a way where I can recall experiences, then put them away and not let them hold me back. EMDR is a fantastic tool, and I highly recommend it for first responders and veterans.

Controlled Breathing

Controlled breathing is a type of breathing exercise that involves concentrating on one's breath and consciously controlling the speed, depth, and pattern of inhalation and exhalation. Controlled breathing is believed to reduce stress and improve feelings of relaxation. It can also help to improve blood pressure and promote improved oxygen levels, as well as reduce symptoms of depression and anxiety.

Breathing exercises help police officers in a few ways. They can provide relaxation and stress relief, improve concentration, increase oxygen flow to the brain, build resilience to stress, and reduce fatigue. They can also be used to refocus during intense situations and to help with emotional regulation. Finally, they can improve response time, helping officers to be better prepared and act more quickly and efficiently in emergency situations.

Show 'em it's COOL to be Well

I touched on this in the leadership chapter, and I can't highlight the importance of **influence** enough. Modeling healthy and effective wellness behaviors is an important part of leadership. By setting an example, leaders have the power to promote healthy habits and attitudes among their team members. This means encouraging healthy habits, such as exercise, proper nutrition, adequate sleep, positive self-talk, vulnerability, and honest communication. Leaders should also be sure to walk the talk and demonstrate such behavior themselves. Doing so can help to promote an atmosphere of healthy behavior, cultivate good attitudes, and inspire team members to perform at their highest potential.

Resilience

I live today with what I would consider "higher levels of resilience." Resilience develops when we experience hard situations and find ways to persevere. Resilience is a loyal friend, but she's not sexy or cool. To become resilient, it simply requires us to do nothing more than acknowledge and embrace our pain. The mistake I made for many years coming home from war and serving my community was working too hard to be comfortable and perfect. I missed chances to become more resilient and respond in the face of adversity. In 2019, I went through a workplace event that required me to tap into my resilience. It was a battle, and I overcame it.

Here is the blueprint I followed (and still deploy) to achieve higher levels of resilience:

1. **Know Thyself**

   Inside and out. Ego focused. Our ego feeds our need to be validated. Strong egos allow for easily corrupted morals. Our egos also play tricks on us, such as the need for positive attention from others. When we seek validation and attention, we become targets in the process. People can manipulate us and expose our desire to serve. Truly knowing ourselves—every part of ourselves (good and bad)—helps us better interact with others. Self-confidence and self-esteem lead to healthy relationships. They also help us establish boundaries with anyone who would do us harm. When we're highly self-aware, it allows us to create situations and opportunities that provide us with energy and momentum. Being self-aware enables us to develop a higher level of resilience.

2. Operate from a Values Structure

Have a code, religion, moral spirit, something of a greater influence. Identify our nonnegotiable values. When we operate from a place of absolute self-knowing in combination with a great source of influence, it creates a level of resilience that we can weather pending storms.

3. Embrace Discomfort

We can only understand ourselves when we fully surrender to the suffering that life provides. With each suffering, we develop deeper resiliency and a higher understanding of ourselves. Identify our most challenging moments and use them as guides to shape our perspectives. Everyone has a personal trauma story they can relate to. These lessons provide us with great opportunities for resilience building. Most of us run away from things that are scary or uncomfortable, but resilience is built for us in those moments.

4. Have a Mission

Having a mission provides us with a framework to handle the unexpected challenges in life. Having a WHY creates momentum, which allows us to move faster and tap into our talents. When we use our talents in the world, it brings us more joy. Joy leads to a healthier lifestyle. Having a mission keeps us centered in community. Storms are inevitable, but they're easier to navigate through when we're set on course.

5. Wellness

Be tenacious with emotional, physical, mental, financial, and spiritual health. No one is going to minimize stress for us. No one is expected to come to our rescue. We must completely take ownership of our life. Without wellness, we cannot regulate our emotions or be the best versions of ourselves. It is impossible to become resilient without being well. All the training, experience, connections, and money will not help us when we're not healthy. We end up wasting all the blessings and talents in our lives if we're not well and healthy. A balanced life and healthy perspectives foster deeper resilience.

Call to Action

When you examine your life and career, write down the parts of your life and values that are nonnegotiable to you. Then, write a separate list of the people in this world you would die for today. Last, make a third list that contains everything you love about yourself. These lists serve as guide rails and a framework. We never deviate from them without cause.

Every morning, with your lists in hand, sit alone in a quiet room for ten minutes a day without distractions. Just ten minutes. During that time, read your lists in **reverse order.** Make a commitment to yourself to do just ten minutes of this self-reflection. Feel free to share what your life looks like in a year.

This exercise is designed to help accurately prioritize the things and people in your life that require our focus and attention. Focusing intently on the most important matters in our life helps us reduce distraction and increase momentum.

ACT III

SPRING

CHAPTER VIIII

CONNECTION!

"WHEN WE ARE NO LONGER ABLE TO CHANGE A SITUATION, WE ARE CHALLENGED TO CHANGE OURSELVES."
~ VIKTOR FRANKL

At the height of the COVID-19 pandemic, I was feeling disconnected from the proud feeling I used to have wearing a police uniform. I was back in patrol, working hard to maintain hope and positivity. I needed additional support with everything I was already doing. I needed more connection!

As police officers, it is essential to have meaningful connections with other officers in order to promote mental and emotional health. Police officers are exposed to extreme circumstances and trauma, which can have a significant impact on their mental and emotional health. Connecting with other officers or community programs can help police officers cope with the demands of their profession and give them a better chance of maintaining positive health outcomes.

I contacted the manager of the local food pantry and asked if I could come in on some off days to help pack meals or do whatever they needed. The manager was kind and gracious about my request. Kristen was off for the summer as a teacher and seemed taken aback by my wanting to volunteer at the food pantry. I guess my behavior appeared irrational. The hard truth was I was lonely—lonely from the love of service I once felt. I was grieving and one way out of the darkness is to do things for others. I arrived for my first shift on an off day. I put on a mask and a hairnet. I was anonymous and didn't tell anyone I was an active-duty police officer. I filled grocery orders, made meals for persons without homes, and met some amazing humans. I volunteered on several different occasions throughout the summer of 2020.

I have many amazing memories from that time volunteering at the food pantry anonymously. A memory that sticks out to me was after packaging meals for the needy, the supervisor on duty asked if I could clean up. She escorted me to the dishwashing station and mop room. I filled the mop bucket and cleaned all the floors. I then cleaned all the dishes, and last took out the trash. In the span of a few hours I made meals for the less fortunate, packaged grocery bags for people that came in needing essentials, and cleaned the facility. A human doing human work. I needed that connection to my community. I needed to be with them more to feel part of it more.

Human Connection?

What is human connection, and what's the big deal? Well, it's important stuff, actually. Human connection are the bonds we form to one another that help us feel seen and heard. Human connection is so significant that if we commit ourselves to each other, connection leads to healthier relationships, less conflict, and higher outputs. We perform better when we're connected to each other!

We have a mental and emotional health crisis in this country. Being unique ought to be celebrated, and I've experienced firsthand how being different is seen as a criticism in policing. Our communities need us to be authentic to who we are. When humans forge strong bonds, I believe there is a transfer of positive energy that eats up most of the problems we face daily. More than anything, humans want to be heard and seen and feel valued and loved.

With every failure and season of discomfort, we have tremendous opportunities to grow and become better versions of ourselves. Instead of running away from our fears and shame, what if we ran directly toward them? I've done so and now share as often as I can with police officers to help them. My life is literally an open book, and I do it begrudgingly for you.

Human connection helps us overcome. I don't want anyone to feel alone. It's scary. We are often the reason we don't overcome our challenges. When we connect with one another and move through the world as collaborators, we foster more opportunities for success and inner peace. This leads to self-confidence and an unwavering commitment to living courageously.

Connection to Reduce Isolation

One of the primary benefits of connection for police officers is the ability to reduce feelings of isolation and loneliness. Police officers often have to spend their days away from family and friends, and their shifts can be extremely isolating. Having meaningful connections with other community stakeholders can help officers feel less alone, and these connections can provide them with a much-needed source of social support.

This topic can trigger some police families who experienced infidelity, but it's another ugly topic we must talk about to improve. In 2022, I had licensed marriage therapist and police spouse Cyndi Doyle on my podcast to discuss this topic. Cyndi found that many police officers cheat on their spouses to feel connected, to feel good. As we learned, it's a core human need to feel safe and protected. When police officers experience trauma and develop poor stress coping strategies, the officer will fall to their foundation of health and training. If cops are not well and don't have a strong set of values and resilience, they are at risk for depression. I experienced it and began withdrawing from social functions. Isolation causes us to commit self-harm and sabotaging behavior.

We must reach out and connect with someone we trust if we're hurting. Trust me, you're not alone in your struggle. Reaching out will lift that burden holding you down. When I confided in my dad about my prescription pill struggle, I still remember the weight being lifted. Together, we can overcome!

Connection Through Communication

Police officers and military personnel can be master communicators when bullets are flying or there's a fatal car crash. We must be strong communicators to get the job done. But what happens when the call is over and we return back to the station? Are we continuing to communicate and engage? What about when one of our teammates is going through a dark season? Why are we so good at communicating on the objective, but some can barely look each other in the eye when there's interpersonal conflict? I think many first responders didn't grow up being shown how to work through conflict.

When they enter service, they are trained and coached on how to do their job. Often, this engagement and structure provide people with low confidence with a heightened level which helps them perform at their job. This new feeling tells many of us that we reached our destination. We achieved that in which we were molded to serve. Maybe it's a little bit of both. When officers have a close interpersonal connection with other police officers, it provides the ability to communicate freely. This is what men need more than anything right now—a safe place to share thoughts and not be ridiculed. To work through conflict and not be judged for emotional responses as they learn how to balance themselves. We are not letting men fail, and many have become afraid or unwilling to communicate honestly.

Police officers can become overwhelmed and stressed out from the pressures of the job, and having a safe space to share their thoughts and feelings can be extremely beneficial. Through communication with other officers, police officers can learn to effectively manage their stress and feelings of anxiety. Such communication can also help officers to recognize the signs of poor mental health in themselves and others and can aid in recovery if necessary.

Connection to Improve Job Performance

Having strong connections with other officers can improve an individual's job performance. Positive communication and relationships among officers can lead to an improved sense of camaraderie, which in turn helps increase job satisfaction. Having stronger relationships between officers can also lead to improved trust and respect, which can help to develop teamwork and increase morale.

Physical Touch

Physical touch has been found to be a helpful way to reduce the stress and trauma police officers are exposed to while on duty. Studies have shown that physical contact, like a hug, handshake, or pat on the back, can trigger the release of endorphins, a natural hormone that has anti-anxiety effects. Physical touch has also been linked to improved mental health, including decreased stress levels, improved cognition, and improved resilience to traumatic events.

Not only is physical contact beneficial for stress management, but it can also help officers achieve greater focus and clarity when resolving a task at hand. The act of touching also conveys trust and comfort, which can help to rebuild positive relationships with colleagues. The combination of these benefits can have a powerful impact in helping individuals to cope with the emotional and psychological stresses of the job.

Physical touch can also provide a safe zone for officers to express themselves without fear of judgment. A reassuring touch from a colleague offers nonverbal communication, which can be cathartic and help to process traumatic events. Studies have found that reassuring physical contact and touch can help foster a feeling of closeness, which can, in turn, establish a greater sense of trust and support for officers working together on a shift.

This topic always makes cops cringe. I'm not advocating committing sexual harassment; rather, I challenge you to incorporate touch as part of your practice. High-fives and fist bumps go a long way to building connection! If a colleague is having a bad day, consider patting or rubbing their back. This is not for everyone, but I do believe through my experiences, this works. I have built close relationships with many cops, and one of the ways I've been able to do it is by being authentic, sincere, and collaborative. Don't be afraid to high-five your buddy—it'll bring you closer!

Positive Psychology

Positive psychology is the study of how people can experience and nurture positive experiences, lead meaningful and fulfilling lives, and build human strengths and resilience in order to promote psychological and emotional well-being. This perspective builds on the idea that individuals are capable of using their own resources to find meaning and success in life. It focuses on studying the positive aspects of life, such as happiness, gratitude, growth, purpose, optimism, courage, and resilience, rather than focusing only on the negative aspects, such as pain, suffering, and fear. Positive psychology looks for ways to help individuals flourish, as opposed to just preventing them from falling into bad psychological states. Through research, practitioners of positive psychology can learn how to encourage and strengthen positive emotions, cultivate helpful traits, and build resilient strategies for coping with life's obstacles.

Here are my top ten things you can do to practice positive psychology:

1. **Self-reflection.** Take time to pause and reflect on your thoughts, feelings, and experiences. Consider how you may be able to grow every day. Visualize the success or inner peace we want and take time to reflect on it. Self-reflection allows us to understand how we affect the world and others around us.
2. **Mindfulness.** Practice mindfulness by being in the present moment. Focus on the here and now and limit rumination about the past or worries about the future. Mindfulness helps us to manage our emotions and validate our feelings. Mindfulness helps us to be in control of external stressors.
3. **Meditation/breathing exercises.** Practice meditative activities such as yoga, tai chi, or other breathing exercises that can help to clear the mind and reduce stress. Focusing on our breath helps us to stay present while also presenting physiological benefits to stress management.
4. **Gratitude.** Cultivate an attitude of gratitude by reflecting on the moments in life that you are thankful for. Make time to express appreciation and thankfulness for your experiences and relationships. We all have things in our lives to be joyful about and upset about. Gratitude is about focusing on the good we have, which helps us build resilience to the bad things we're dealing with.

5. **Exercise.** Participate in daily physical activity to increase mood-boosting endorphins. Exercise is mandatory in order for us to be joyful and healthy.

6. **Positive affirmations.** Use positive affirmations to retrain your thoughts and change negative thinking patterns. Speak out-loud positive statements such as "I am capable" and "I can do hard things." By speaking positively to ourselves, we curate the narrative for us to operate from. Affirming others also has tremendous benefits for connection and resilience. Police cultures struggle mightily in this area.

7. **Journaling.** Taking time to write down your thoughts and experiences can help to uncover new levels of your self-worth and understanding. My sixth-grade English teacher Mr. Lagrotte handed me a black-and-white composition book, and I've been journaling ever since. Journaling has had such a profound effect on my emotional and mental well-being that I'm not sure where I'd be today without it.

8. **Acts of kindness.** Make a habit of performing acts of kindness for yourself and your community. When we do selfless things for others without attention or expectations, we are providing value to the world. We fill our emotional cup by connecting with others and serving them where they're at.

9. **Cognitive reframing.** Challenge yourself to reframe negative thoughts and behaviors into positive ones. Practicing this process can help to break the cycle of negative thinking. A technique to do this is practicing recapitulation. *Recapitulation* is the practice of replaying or summarizing the primary points or facts of something to help us gain clarity. When we replay events in our head, we tend to focus on the good things that happened to us throughout the day. Combining recapitulation with mindfulness on a consistent basis has healing effects on our emotional health.

10. **Setting goals.** Identify specific, achievable goals and work toward accomplishing them. Celebrate the small victories as well as the big ones. Without a goal or vision, we are rudderless ships waiting on a wind gust to move us. We can't expect others to save us or help us. We take control by setting challenging goals and committing ourselves to executing them. Setting reasonable expectations goes a long way toward curbing disappointment. Goals should be challenging, not impossible. Goals can be reset and moved. The focus is to keep moving toward our destination.

Likability

Likability is one of the most important yet underrated characteristics of successful police officers. Not only does likeability help to build trust between officers and the communities they serve, but it also has a number of intrinsic benefits for police officers themselves.

When we're likable police officers, we can expect some of the following benefits:

1. **Less stress.** Police officers face an immense amount of stress on a daily basis. Working in a high-pressure environment can have serious implications not only for their health but also for their performance on the job. Being likable in the community and in our teams helps to reduce stress, as officers are better able to build positive relationships with those they encounter in the community.

2. **More compliance, less use of force.** Being likable can help a police officer better gain compliance from citizens. When officers are likable, they come across as friendly, approachable, and trustworthy. This can make people more likely to listen and comply with police commands and requests. Having friendly interactions with citizens can also build a sense of community and trust between police officers and the people they serve, which can increase the likelihood of

compliance during future interactions. When officers are likable, it can often help diffuse tense or volatile situations by providing an emotionally safe environment in which people can interact calmly and respectfully with a police officer, thus helping to avoid conflict.

3. **Increased performance.** A likable officer is better able to interact with people and build trust. This helps to ensure that calls are handled promptly, community safety is upheld, and established relationships with citizens are maintained. This increases the effectiveness of police officers and strengthens the bond between the officer and the community. Likable officers become more credible in their community, and that leads to higher outputs for the officer.

4. **Career advancement.** People are naturally drawn to those who they like. As such, a likable police officer is more likely to be promoted within the force, as well as more likely to receive commendations or awards. This is an important consideration for those looking to rise through the ranks within their police force. Collaboration increases as we become likable, which leads to higher levels of connection and job satisfaction.

5. **Safer working environment.** A likable officer is less likely to be targeted by those in the community who wish to do harm to police officers. Officers who have unlikable personalities and carry shame are more likely to be assaulted or targeted. Likable officers generally place importance on human connection and therefore develop higher levels of resilience.

Personal Branding for Police?

> "If likability is so cool, then why don't we use it more in the course of our role as police officers?"

That was the question I asked myself as I watched his awesome presentation. In 2021, I attended a seminar by Louisiana State

University Professor Dr. Tommy Karam. Dr. Karam helps the sports media department at LSU with his knowledge based on personal branding. He has worked with collegiate and professional athletes, such as Shaquille O'Neal. Dr. Karam has studied **likability** and found it to be the most common reason people agree to do business with us and our best weapon for a successful negotiation. Likability! Think about it from the lens of a police officer. Just by being more likable, we're more likely to get people (aka citizens) to enter into business (aka compliance) with us. Interesting, Dr. Karam. But how does this work?

Dr. Karam's studies were actually in the larger context of *personal branding*. Dr. Karam has three basic tenants of personal branding for the athlete to successfully negotiate and speak with the media.

- *The camera never blinks.* People are always looking at you, even when the cameras are off. You've got to be aware of people looking at you.
- *The thin slice.* It's all about little moments people remember forever, the 1/20th of a second, the short moment when people make a judgment of you.
- *The default look.* The expression you have when you're not paying attention to how you look.

As I sat in Dr. Karam's seminar, the question that I had been asking in my head changed to an emphatic statement.

This is what policing needs! I will bring personal branding to them, I passionately thought. Most cops don't smile and cross their arms. We often don't appear approachable, and our default look isn't friendly. By posturing tactically and unfriendly for the potential attack, we're alienating ourselves from the majority of the citizens we deal with who are law-abiding citizens.

Here's my challenge to you: smile more! Don't fold your arms as much, and take your sunglasses off when you're talking to someone. Let them see your eyes. Let them see your teeth. Let them see your heart. None of those things will cause you physical harm on the street, but they will help you gain compliance and build strong relationships in the community.

I Want to Love Myself: Network, Net Worth, Self-Worth

People and money are the two quickest ways for us to feel loved. Do we have a lot of friends and money? If so, we made it—we're successful! Generationally, we've mentored young people to build strong networks because they help you get people who will help you get money. So we enter into the regimen of shaking hands, giving awkward introductions, inauthentic team-building approaches, and more, all because we were told that's what makes us successful.

It's true. A social and professional network is important because it helps to build relationships, increase visibility, broaden business opportunities, and keep up with industry trends. By connecting with relevant people and organizations, a person or company can gain access to potential partners, collaborators, investors, clients, and resources. In addition, staying connected via a social and professional network can help a person or business stay informed and competitive in their industry. Nothing untrue about any of that. Let's go where people stop.

Relationships and connections are vital for our sense of belonging. Why do we stop investing in professional relationships when there's interpersonal conflict? Conflict is part of life, so we must learn to work through it. Otherwise, we'll be 80 with no one left to fight with. What if we flip our mindsets to focus on making relationships a priority? What if we never lie to a teammate or betray them? What would happen if we focused on adding value to every citizen we meet? What would our life look like if we committed ourselves to living and serving with intention and purpose?

I challenge you to search for people who are completely opposite to you. By doing this, you will build an eclectic network that is equally loyal to you. By building healthy relationships and setting boundaries, the power of the network will be in full force. One person can be marginalized, discredited, or hurt. It is quite difficult to stand in the way of a powerful network of selfless and team-minded people with values. Where one person is deficient, another in the network is an expert. When one of the most intellectual people in the network can't work through a human relations issue, strong networks can tap into the empaths who can take the lead and massage the chaos.

Teams with a mix of personalities, interests, values, ideologies, and beliefs are to be celebrated! Too many police departments and organizations have built teams that won't challenge the status quo or speak up in a way to make the overall system better. We've largely created systems with the same thought process. We don't want different or challenging. That's un-American to me and, more importantly, counterproductive to the process of becoming **excellent**. The journey toward excellence is never ending, and we will need many allies to join our fight. As police organizations, we want to be excellent, right? To become excellent, we must understand the rules of the game. Understanding the rules and preparing to win increases our chances of winning the hearts and minds within our communities.

I caution you to properly identify all of these terms so you can put them in the proper place:

Network

Net worth

Self-worth

We just talked about networking and its importance. Let's move on to the others. These are tricky, and for many of us, we have blurred them so dysfunctional that many of us have lost personal relationships because we couldn't make this distinction.

Net worth and self-worth are closely related but are not the same. Net worth is an indication of the value of your assets and liabilities, while self-worth is an assessment of your personal value. Many people consciously or subconsciously view net worth as an indicator of their own worth, so they confuse the two concepts. This is especially true in societies where wealth and status are given special attention or importance, like the United States.

Our capitalistic system has linked "success" to "earnings." It's really a shame if we reflect. How many of us hurt ourselves and others in the pursuit of "success"? From politicians to professional athletes, we conditioned ourselves to use a piece of paper as a measuring stick. No wonder we have a mental and emotional health crisis in this country. We're like squirrels chasing nuts, and very few of us are carrying the majority of the nuts.

As a coach, I challenge you to focus on impact and purpose. When we engage in living a life of significance by serving others, the intrinsic earning power we receive from the mission helps to place financial earnings in the proper place. There is beauty in working hard and creating something. There is pride in being compensated for it. Isn't that just one factor? How many wealthy brothers and sisters are sitting in their house right now, hitting the bottle or blasting a line of cocaine, trying to figure out their next move? How many friends did we lose along this journey?

When we continually burn bridges, it can lead to a lack of trust and difficulty in forming and maintaining relationships. Additionally, this can lead to isolation from others and, ultimately, a feeling of loneliness. People may also experience career and economic hardships as their reputation begins to suffer and they are unable to make professional connections. The long-term effects of continually placing financial earnings at the forefront of professional success is that it can be damaging both socially and professionally.

What if we build a strong foundation in life first, then attack our dreams? It seems unrealistic and unsustainable to pursue riches and not take hostages along the way. What happens if you're one of the lucky ones who makes it? Are there people who love you by your side to celebrate with you? Or is there an emptiness that sits in your belly that gets you mad just thinking about it? I know that feeling. Make a choice to heal. You can do it!

What Does This All Mean?

I don't think an officer can survive and thrive in a full career without strong connections. The fewer connections we have, the more we risk mental and emotional health problems over a period of time. Connection is essential for all police officers in order to maintain their mental and emotional health. Without strong connections, police officers are more likely to harm themselves. Police officers kill themselves drastically more than the community kills them. By building positive connections with other officers through communication and trust, police officers can reduce feelings of isolation, sharpen their communication skills, and ultimately, improve job performance. Connection can help police officers to cope with the demands of their profession and can be a valuable tool for maintaining positive health outcomes.

Let's resist being perfect and focus on reducing the harm happening to our officers by connecting, engaging, sharing, and growing together!

The Bank of Good Credit

One of the most important things to help build a strong and peaceful community is to foster meaningful connections between police and community members. Police officers are tasked with keeping everyone, regardless of race, gender, or identity, safe and protected. By cultivating strong relationships between them and the community, people of all backgrounds can have trust and faith in their local police department.

Can a police department have a close relationship with the community if officers are not well? Of course, they can't! Unwell officers are unable to positively contribute to the community due to their own pain. What happens if the chief executive is unwell? I think you can answer that for yourself by now.

Police officers and community members must work together to find solutions to challenges in order to support each other, whether this is through developing youth initiatives or brainstorming ways to help the vulnerable. Open conversations and trust-building activities, such as community gardens, urban green spaces, or volunteering events, offer a safe space to foster these meaningful connections. It's essential to ensure that all members of the community, including the police force, have a voice heard and respected.

Many police departments offer "coffee and a cop," and while those are good for community engagement, they're only scratching the surface of what could be. What if agencies started scheduling monthly community events with the sole intention of building relationships? Wow, that's inspiring.

The point of all of this is to build up a morally strong brank account of goodwill. The better police departments forge relationships in the community, the less conflict they will have. The closer police departments are aligned to the fabric of the community, there will be less divide and more collaboration.

I heard my entire career that police departments should hire more from the community they serve. That's a noble effort and I have no issue with it – however wouldn't another option be to hire cops based on their emotional intelligence than their written test scores and how they answer tactical questions on an oral board. Many agencies are simply hiring the wrong type of human being.

I believe in the power of positive relationships and when both sides are on equal footing, amazing collaborative opportunities arise. Together, police officers and community members can create a peaceful and vibrant community that's rooted in mutual respect and understanding.

Call to Action

When I'm feeling down or need inspiration, I do random acts of kindness for people. Strangers. Watching another human experience joy makes me feel better. The beauty of random acts of kindness is that our actions directly bring someone else joy and happiness. It's more than being nice to people; it's about being connected to virtue and sharing that connection with another person.

Humans desire gratification. We engage in behaviors that cause our emotional state to improve. So, if you're unable to change your depressed condition, try helping a stranger. Buy them dinner or hold the door for them. When we foster human interactions that cause smiles, our self-worth improves. We feel valuable and purposeful. Want to feel better in life? Help someone. Do something kind for someone. By adding value to the lives of others, we essentially are rewiring our brains to be more grateful and positive. We are literally becoming the change we want to see in the world. We're leading by example and demonstrating our authenticity for other officers to give witness to.

When you retire, what legacy do you want to leave? What do you want cops to say about you? I know you care because our actions show that we care greatly about the opinions of others. Serve others consistently and watch your life change. Smile more and watch your relationships improve. Listen more and see how many more people start calling you. Give more than you take, and you'll be surprised that by being humble and sacrificial, you'll receive more blessings than you ever thought possible. We think the harder we work, the better our chances are at succeeding. I don't think that's a true statement necessarily; it's a rather lazy correlation.

I can attest to this unequivocally: the more we love, the better our chances are succeeding; however we define success. What's holding you back from loving people more?

CHAPTER X

REIMAGINING

"TWO ROADS DIVERGED IN A WOOD AND I TOOK THE ONE LESS TRAVELED BY, AND THAT HAS MADE ALL THE DIFFERENCE."
-ROBERT FROST

From Blue to Gray: Criminal Justice Reimagined

The reality inside the policing profession that we struggle to acknowledge in a society of law and order is that few things are black and white. Policing is a messy profession. From the citizens we deal with to our own dysfunctional lives, police are on the front lines of community trauma. Instead of police officers casting judgment or judges exacting justice according to their personal beliefs, the criminal justice system is broken. We're releasing violent criminals on the streets and over-punishing hardworking Americans. The system is broken but we don't have to tear it down completely. The criminal justice system, like a business, needs an injection of new leadership with unique voices. Imagine if we created a criminal justice system where people with lived experiences were in leadership roles. When we create multi-disciplined and eclectic teams, criminal justice agencies can better relate and serve our citizens. Policing is collaborative, not authoritative.

We've been conditioned in society to believe there's only one way to do something. In reality, there are multiple methods for each task that generally provide similar outcomes, yet each method is as unique as the other. Often in police work and in the military, we subscribe to the easiest measures to accomplish the task. Leadership is one area in which we should always chase uniqueness. So many of us are focused on always making the right decisions. It's become a right versus wrong proposition. Black and white. Vanilla and chocolate.

Systematically, we've watered down the individual uniqueness of leaders. Our cultures largely stopped celebrating being different, and many of us are carbon copies of our bosses. This type of rigidness and copycatting has hurt the profession in major ways. Primarily, the world is very gray and the policing profession has seemingly become a profession where only black and white is accepted. Leading differently has not just been unheralded in many police agencies; police leaders leading in unique ways have reported being targeted for their varying styles in how they lead. I subscribed to a virtue-based leadership style. I focus on modeling proper behavior, being present for my teams, and leading with love. How many police and military leaders are punished for their virtue and for leading differently than others?

I spent twenty-one years in police and military cultures. I served in numerous and varying professional organizational cultures during that time. For my purposes, each new company commander or chief of police brings a fresh and distinct leadership perspective and represents separate cultures. Organizational culture is established by the chief executive of the organization. Those are unique command structures, each having its own identity and philosophies. Each culture led in different manners and subscribed to varying leadership styles.

Gray Area Leadership

Leading others in the gray area is a real challenge. The gray area refers to an uncertain, ambiguous situation with no clear right or wrong options. It's a situation where there may be high stakes, and the risk of making the wrong decision is high. As a leader, it's important to have the capacity to balance and handle the pressures of the gray area. Gray areas scare the heck out of leaders. Whenever we have to go off-script, we are grossly uncomfortable with things we don't understand. By not embracing discomfort, we rarely learn new things and we continue the cycle of only scratching the surface of our leadership potential. The real secret of highly influential leaders is that they meet their teammates where they're at, and they learn how to push through their fears and insecurities due to their passion for serving others. They *love* to get muddy.

Here are some tips on how to lead others in the gray area:

1. **Understand the situation.** Before making a decision, take time to fully understand the situation and the people involved. Collect as many facts and perspectives as possible from those involved and from outside sources. Actively listen and do not judge or offer feedback. Allow yourself to process all the information. We don't always need rushed solutions. Sometimes the best thing we can do is nothing at first. Keeping an open mind when gathering information and spotting any potential pitfalls will allow you to make a more informed decision. There's nothing wrong with telling a teammate, "I want to best help you. Please give me a short period of time as I focus on the solution." This was another way of saying, "I don't know, but I will find out."

2. **Define the risk.** Evaluate the risks and potential costs associated with different solutions to the problem. Reassess the risks on a regular basis as new information arises. Don't be afraid to be unique. The most effective leaders aren't paralyzed by risk. If you end up routinely festering on your own liability, then it will be difficult to curry influence. Influence is selfless by nature, and therefore our own risks should be the only concern we're thinking about. Worrying about our own consequences keeps us from being influential and impactful.

3. **Seek input.** Invite different community stakeholders, team members, and other interested parties to offer their input and provide more insight into the situation. This will help you make a more comprehensive and balanced decision. Leadership is a team sport; we don't have to take on all the burdens of leadership alone. Leadership is collaborative, and highly skilled leaders understand they're only as effective as the teamwork they solicit. Each day leaders should be receiving feedback from our teams on how to best make a

difference. If our teammates stop providing routine feedback, it could be a sign of a toxic environment. Ineffective leaders may say, "My team never complains, so we're good," when in reality, the lack of free-flow communication tends to be a sign of unhealthy cultures.

4. **Planning.** Set clear expectations and guidelines that will guide the team and the decision-making process. Make sure everyone is on the same page and understands the goals and aims of the project. Having clear expectations allows leaders to lead their teams from the margins. Fear should not be a part of leadership decisions.

    My expertise in leadership and culture allows me to see past the personal and unhealthy decisions of leaders. When I was "demoted," it was the day after I made two felony arrests for attempted homicide. We provided safety to the community and did this routinely. The reassignment of detectives from patrol wasn't cooperative. I was surprised by the move, and the chief and lieutenant sitting on one side of the table and me sitting on the other side felt more punitive than collaborative. There was no speech on how this move benefits the agency or community. It was short, sweet, and direct. It's not how you treat an integral member of the agency.

    Furthermore, I went from detective to officer. I was told to turn in all my detective badges and cell phone. There was no discussion; these were orders sent via email and text. Each time I approached the chief and lieutenant for a discussion, I was told, "You'll be back in detectives within a year." Twelve months later, they stopped saying that. The whole move was painfully confusing to many people as the chief continued to tell stakeholders, "It's good for the department."

    The cold hard truth that should keep the mayor, council, and residents up at night is that the community and agency suffered tremendously when Chief Pathe made those personal decisions to demote Nick and me. He did it for himself, no matter what he says. His arrogance hurts the community, yet like many selfish leaders, they work hard to craft a narrative that they're collaborative and service minded. In reality, these kinds of leaders actually punish people with service-minded personalities because the virtue of these public servants is a direct reminder of their own glowing deficiencies. You can't pretend to be virtuous when you're around truly virtuous people. Those leaders need to create an environment where they're the most virtuous.

5. **Know your teammates.** Leaders must know each team member to understand what motivates them. Leaders must be able to adjust to unexpected situations with their team members and make constant adjustments as new information becomes available. Show your team that you're capable of developing unique solutions to problems. Don't be afraid to be different! Your uniqueness is what others will attack because of their insecurities of being ordinary; and their fears of failing. You cannot fall victim to this mindset, as it will destroy your virtue. **Virtue** is what sets effective leaders apart from ineffective leaders.

Differentiated Leadership

Our teammates require varying levels of leadership. Some are disciplined and passionate. They need less guidance than other teammates. Other teammates are dealing with problems at home and require a deeper level of care. As leaders, we must identify each individual teammate's needs and meet them where they're at. A fatal flaw for leaders is when they treat their teammates the same. In policing, too many leaders are worried about liability and were not developed properly to be comfortable leading in the gray area. Our profession is failing in our ability to nurture, develop, and prepare leaders.

Leading others in the gray area can be challenging. It is far easier to treat all team members the same than to differentiate leadership styles. Leaders are missing tremendous opportunities to connect with everyone on their team. By staying open-minded, keeping an eye on the risks, and seeking input from different sources, you can make rational, informed decisions.

In 2001, while pursuing a promotion to sergeant at 20 in the Army, I attended a thirty-day residency leadership school, Primary Leadership Development Course. I learned a lot about leadership and the varying leadership modalities. Our cadre informed us to pick one leadership style and stick with it. It was simple enough for a novice like me to learn. Over the next two decades of leading in dynamic roles, I learned that deploying only one leadership style was not only improper but also limiting. The world is dynamic, and often humans are faced with nonlinear challenges. Leadership is the same way: influencing others toward a common goal is challenging.

I recommend you try every leadership style possible. Being a chameleon when serving in leadership roles allows us to better connect to everyone on our teams. Leading in the gray area is nothing more than meeting your team members where they're at.

Leading people in a gray area can be a difficult task. This type of leadership requires the ability to be able to effectively balance competing needs and interests, negotiate and resolve conflicts, and create workable solutions to challenges posed by ambiguity and uncertainty. I have found that when leaders successfully navigate the gray area with their teammates, it leads to lower turnover, higher resilience, and larger outcomes.

Leaders who constantly operate in the gray area are required to think and act strategically. This kind of leadership requires more than just operational management. Leaders must be able to analyze a situation and then make decisions based on their understanding of the complexity and uncertainty of the issues at hand. It is not sufficient to simply make a decision based on a set of predetermined rules or outcomes. Instead, the leader must think critically and consider all of the factors at play before making a decision. This strategic thinking benefits both the organization and the individual.

Leading in the gray area encourages critical problem-solving. Problems faced in the gray area are often complex and convoluted. Leaders operating in this environment must be able to break the problem down into manageable chunks in order to achieve the desired results. This kind of problem-solving is essential in any organization and can have a long-term impact on business success.

Additionally, leading in the gray area allows leaders to foster creative solutions. This kind of leadership also encourages experimentation and allows for flexibility in finding the best solution. Gray Area Leaders are not afraid to fail because they have learned that the real lessons of impact are out on the margins. The pursuit of trying new things encourages employees to think outside the box when faced with complex obstacles, which can lead to breakthrough innovations.

Solutions

Collaboration significantly improves when we lead others in the gray areas. Working in a gray area requires compromise and negotiation to reach a consensus. This encourages a team approach that can help to build trust between both the leader and the followers. It also encourages a culture of open communication and mutual respect that can be invaluable to any organization.

I argue that repairing police cultures isn't enough. We need to grow and adapt. Change is hard, and it's required to be the best version of our noble profession.

Here are my recommendations for five improvements that criminal justice agencies can begin to implement immediately:

1. **Implement data-driven and evidence-based policing methods.** Adopting data-driven and evidence-based policing methods that embrace modern technology can help law enforcement agencies identify patterns and prevent crime. By utilizing data-driven analytics and predictive technologies, police departments can more effectively focus their resources and better target high-risk areas and individuals.

2. **Develop stronger community relationships.** Police officers should strive to build positive relationships with the

communities they serve. Law enforcement agencies should work to bridge the gap between police and the public through increased awareness, education, outreach, and dialogue. Foster contacts and empathize with the citizens in the communities they serve instead of relying solely on aggressive tactics in order to build trust and show respect. When we have stronger bonds in the community and lead with love, we can overcome any challenge that presents itself in our communities. Collaboration is paramount.

3. **Enhance oversight and accountability.** Establishing clear and transparent policies and procedures is needed to ensure accountability and reduce misconduct. This includes creating internal systems to review use-of-force policies and practices, as well as reviewing citizen complaints. By strengthening oversight, police departments can help restore public confidence in the profession and create an environment where trust and respect are possible. This includes the executive team of every agency. Leaders, more than rank-and-file officers, must be held accountable and remain transparent and neutral.

4. **Increase diversity.** Police departments need to actively recruit and hire a more diverse population that is reflective of the communities they serve. By increasing the diversity of law enforcement, police departments can better mirror the communities they serve, thereby fostering greater trust and respect. This is challenging in smaller communities, and police agencies could benefit from recruiting outside of the box.

5. **Improve training and organizational culture.** Police departments need to provide more comprehensive and specialized training that will help officers better handle situations that involve people in distress, de-escalate volatile situations, and better understand minority cultures. Officers should be trained to handle confrontations and conflicts in a more collaborative and nonconfrontational

way. The more agencies develop their officers, the better prepared they will be to respond appropriately to the challenging and dynamic environments that our communities present. We must be emotionally more stable than the citizens we serve, and over the past decade and a half, I've seen the mental and emotional state of many officers decline lower than the citizens we serve.

Community Responder Program

For the thirteen years I was a police officer, I rarely enjoyed responding to low-level calls while I was trying to write a narcotics search warrant or type up a robbery arrest warrant. I was focused on large-impact activities, and while I loved interacting with the community, I believed police officers should spend their time doing what they're the best at. That's how we transcend communities. As policing evolves, we should continue to examine all possible solutions to gauge their viability and beta test ones that warrant the effort. This is what the process of getting great at something looks like. No egos, selfless teamwork, and a relentless pursuit toward excellence.

In cities across our nation, police departments are facing a significant challenge in maintaining adequate staffing levels. Meanwhile, our 9-1-1 call centers are inundated with low-level calls that do not necessarily require an armed police response. These calls encompass issues such as noise complaints, loitering, nuisance calls, ordinance violations, as well as mental and behavioral health concerns. As a result, our law enforcement resources are stretched thin, and valuable time and energy are being diverted away from addressing more serious crimes.

I have been fortunate to work on a volunteer basis for the Law Enforcement Action Partnership (LEAP), a nonprofit organization that works to "unite and mobilize the voice of law enforcement in support of drug policy and criminal justice reforms that will make communities safer by focusing law enforcement resources on the greatest threats to public safety, promoting alternatives to arrest and incarceration, addressing the root causes of crime, and working toward healing police-community relations."

This is where community responder programs come into play. LEAP has been actively advocating and collaborating with cities nationwide to implement these programs, which have proven to be highly effective tools in public safety response. By leveraging the expertise of well-trained professionals, community responders can offer an appropriate and targeted response to these low-level calls, freeing up our police officers to focus on more pressing matters. I suppose that most patrol officers and administrations would prefer to have their officers ready and prepared for emergency calls.

So, what exactly are community responders? They are unarmed teams of professionals who serve as true first responders, arriving at the scene before the police have even cleared it. These professionals undergo extensive training in mediation, conflict resolution, and mental and behavioral health, enabling them to handle a wide range of situations. It's important to note that community responder teams do not include armed officers, as they differ from co-responder teams in this regard.

Numerous cities in the U.S., such as Eugene, Dayton, Albuquerque, Olympia, Austin, Durham, and many more, have already embraced this innovative approach to public safety. It's early and there are reasons to believe that these cities will have success with their programs. An effective program would ensure that citizens receive the appropriate level of care and assistance promptly while allowing our police force to focus their resources where they are most needed.

LEAP is doing great work to bring new voices to the criminal justice reform space. One of the initiatives that LEAP supports, and so do I, is **Community Responder** programs. The following information is provided by the LEAP organization. I have built a relationship with Executive Director and retired Police Lieutenant Diane Goldstein, and she is passionate about making real changes in the interest of communities.

Today, local elected officials are increasingly facing calls to reduce reliance on police to respond to calls for service. Indeed, data clearly demonstrate that law enforcement is often dispatched to address 911 calls that could be more appropriately handled by civilians—a situation that is detrimental to community members and officers alike. By adopting a Community Responder model, cities have an opportunity to reduce the volume of calls to which police must respond, mitigating the negative impacts that can result from an overreliance on policing. Community Responders, with their intensive training and lived experiences with the issues facing communities, are uniquely positioned to provide an effective solution to answering calls for service that do not require a law enforcement response.

Ultimately, a Community Responder program operates with a vision of helping communities resolve problems internally without the justice system. Public safety is about more than just policing; when residents experience crime or disorder, they should have tools beyond the police at their disposal. Americans understand this: A recent survey found that nearly 8 in 10 voters support diverting mental health- and substance use-related 911 calls to trained, nonpolice responders. The goal of the CR model is to ensure that every neighborhood has the resources to settle more disturbances and disputes and find long-term solutions outside of the justice system to recurring public safety issues.

As with any new initiative, the Community Responder model may face initial skepticism. Yet the best evidence for the model is to see it in action. Six months after the CRU model was implemented in Olympia, a survey of law enforcement showed that many veteran officers had already gone from skeptics to champions of the model. One officer explained that he had been called to respond to the same individuals over and over for 20 years, and he assumed he would be doing it until he retired. Suddenly, the CRU responders not only took those calls off of his plate but also helped find long-term solutions that worked for the people involved, so much so that the community no longer called about them.

Safety is a concern, and the primary risk to safety is the fact that community responder units will not be armed or trained for violence. As I learned more about community responder units, I became increasingly optimistic about the sustainability of these programs. They're effective and remarkably safe. I think we will learn after more data is collected that a team of trained responders made up of community members can be effective at building relationships, resolving conflict, and de-escalation.

Community responder programs have been in existence for quite some time, with the oldest and most renowned program located in Eugene, Oregon. CAHOOTS (Crisis Assistance Helping Out On The Streets) is a mobile crisis intervention program staffed by White Bird Clinic personnel using City of Eugene vehicles. This relationship has been in place for nearly thirty years and is well-embedded in the community. CAHOOTS provides support for EPD personnel by taking on many of the social service type calls for service, including crisis counseling. CAHOOTS personnel often provide initial contact and transport for people who are intoxicated, mentally ill, or disoriented, as well as transport for necessary nonemergency medical care.

Remarkably, in all these years, not a single responder has been lost or seriously injured while answering a call in Eugene. Unarmed professionals engage with the public every day in various capacities, such as social workers and other city employees who respond to calls. With the right protocols and comprehensive training, we can ensure the safety of our community responders. This training will encompass techniques on arriving safely, assessing a scene, and effectively utilizing police radio to call for backup when needed.

In 2021, CAHOOTS saved the City of Eugene Police Department between 3–8% of call responses. That's more time for police officers to focus and deploy strategic resources that will make us more efficient while improving relationships with those we serve, like I did for all those years. The community responder program is a great model for cities or agencies not interested in cross-training their officers or developing a co-responder program.

As a former undercover narcotics officer and detective, I wanted to focus on my duties and perform them at the highest levels. Momentum is key for high performers. Community Responder programs are not a defund-the-police initiative for those who have concerns about your position. Is there a potential for community responder programs to reduce the need for police officers? Maybe. Only time will show.

Here's what I know as a retired cop who loves policing: the United States needs armed and trained police officers. Have you consciously thought about what America would look like without armed and trained police officers? I have, and it's a scary thought. There's no way around the fact that we must have police officers in our communities, and that's a beautiful thing. But we don't need to handle every call for service. There should be no ego from executives on this topic because chiefs don't own the police department, the community does. The relationship between the police department and the community is collaborative and fluid. No one should be in charge because it's not about authority, yet most police agencies have turned community service into authority.

If policing wants to be excellent, then we ought to consider every approach to becoming masters of our profession. Implementing trained citizens to carry the load with the officers is collaborative and inspiring. Instead of one or another, I challenge agencies to incorporate both. We become excellent by demonstrating "can do" attitudes.

I know policing "can do" this.

The Cop Avatar

This may be controversial to many cops currently in the field, and my mission is to include—not ostracize. However, I must remain honest about the facts plaguing our profession. The policing profession has been hiring and promoting the wrong candidate for decades, which led us to where we are. It's really that simple. In any job, if we don't form the right teams, chances are we won't be successful at our job. Below are the traits and characteristics we should be screening for. Communities require a specific type of human to serve them.

Traits that make the best police officers are:

- Commitment to others
- Integrity
- Strong communication skills
- Empathy
- A calm demeanor (emotionally balanced)
- Sound judgment
- Adaptability
- Problem-solving abilities
- Good self-control
- Physically fit
- Humble
- EQ
- Person with passion

Commitment is a key trait of an ideal police officer. They should be dedicated to protecting the public and upholding the law. They should also be committed to their job and be willing to go the extra mile when necessary. We do extra when we're passionate about serving others. Integrity is also essential in law enforcement. Police officers must always make sure their behavior is above reproach and that they adhere to the highest ethical standards.

Strong **communication** skills are also important for police officers in order to effectively deal with difficult situations. They need to be able to listen carefully to understand the situation and take into account the perspectives of both the suspect and the victim.

Empathy is necessary for officers to be able to understand different perspectives and gain the trust and cooperation of those they interact with. Being able to empathize with different individuals and communities is essential to successful policing. There are thousands of police officers serving with little or no empathy and it's ruining the profession. Policing must not be treated like a business.

Good **self-control** is also essential for police officers in order to remain calm in tense situations and not act out of anger or haste. Police officers need to be able to maintain their composure even in difficult and chaotic situations. The lack of consistent emotional health is affecting many police officers and communities.

Physical fitness is also critical for police officers. Officers need to be in good physical condition in order to be able to protect themselves and others, chase suspects, and detain them if necessary. Full-spectrum wellness is mandatory for police officers. Sound judgment is also essential for police officers to make decisions quickly and responsibly. They should be able to draw on past experiences and training in order to assess and respond to the best of their ability.

Law enforcement has placed an emphasis on SWAT operators and undercover officers. It's sexy and fun. But it's not policing. I've seen chiefs with poor leadership skills be promoted because of their reputation as a great SWAT officer or because they effectuated many arrests. The benchmarks we're using are flawed and it's another reason the profession is broken. Instead, what if we focused on leadership merits? Leaders are not supposed to be the smartest people in the room, and it's the egos of unhealthy leaders that perpetuate this belief.

Leaders are facilitators and doers. They're not geniuses. They have a vision, understand how teams collaborate, communicate at high levels, and put the right teammates in the right positions to succeed. Nothing is personal and everything is about the team. Policing has become a profession of self-righteous, binge drinking, unhealthy citizens trying to police more unhealthy citizens.

CHAPTER XI

RETENTION

RECRUITMENT

"YOU SEE THINGS; AND YOU SAY 'WHY?' BUT I DREAM THINGS THAT NEVER WERE; AND I SAY 'WHY NOT?'"
-GEORGE BERNARD SHAW

Fixing Police Retention and Recruitment

"You know we'll fill your seat as soon as you leave," was a comment made by my lieutenant in 2019. I was back in patrol, and we were talking about valuing employees and showing them all more respect. I could have conversations with our lieutenant then. That's when he said this line. You know what? He couldn't be more wrong, but it was the culture he was raised in. I reject this belief that many police leaders also believe. This is lazy, ineffective leadership. Agencies can fill spots, but they can't duplicate cops. The mere comment is what drives good cops to leave, devaluing them to the point where you're telling them they're replaceable while they're employed there. How does this help the morale of our officers who are already dealing with so much?

Some Numbers

As a police life coach with Axon's Performance Protocol, I was startled to learn the recruitment and retention numbers. According to P2's research, from 2019-2021, these were the following statistics:

24% - increase in resignations

43% - increase in retirements

67% - decrease in applications

While we can point our fingers at many reasons for this, I pose this question for you to consider: If an agency has a chief executive who's created a culture of the following, why would any police officer want to leave?

- Inclusion
- Fairness
- Merit-based
- People-focused

The reality is that officers leave organizations because of people-related issues; the job itself is only one factor. It always comes back to the actual people wearing the uniform in the administrative offices. Do they have character and honor? Are they ethical and moral? These are mandatory requirements for leadership.

The Great Resignation

Ask any HR director and they'll tell you it's much more cost-efficient to **retain** teammates than recruit them. I was an expert in multiple areas and was one of the highest-performing cops in the department. Moreover, I cared a great deal about serving the community. Due to the personal nature of my demotion, when I submitted my retirement paperwork, there wasn't one conversation about me staying. The agency was letting one of their top performers go without a simple conversation. It was another affirmation that the very nature of my demotion and subsequent departure was rooted in personal vindictiveness.

Another officer from my agency left in 2023 after approximately six years. Pennsylvania doesn't have a lateral transfer program or statewide pension system. This young officer is bright and talented. He was a DARE officer and had other responsibilities. The agency invested in him like they did me. This officer left the agency and gave up six years of retirement time and started the clock over. I assume this officer left due to culture, and I also assume that this officer wasn't honest about his departure. When we're serving in unhealthy cultures, honesty and transparency are difficult to come by.

Generally, when employees leave a job, it's because of the people and not the job itself. We have to start better treating our officers like the professionals and talented individuals they are. That's how we keep better cops in the ranks. Haven't our communities earned to be served by the best of us? The real rub to retaining our team members is by leaders being better people. By leaders better serving and appreciating their teams, the good employees with other opportunities may elect to stay and be loyal to a mission and department that's loyal to them.

The COVID-19 pandemic and the economic situation for many American families largely drove the great resignation in 2020. As businesses closed and layoffs spread across the country, many workers had no other choice but to resign from their positions due to their financial difficulties. Additionally, health concerns, childcare needs, and the closure of many school and college programs left many workers feeling that their current positions were no longer viable options. In addition, people started waking up and taking stock of their lives. It created an opportunity to pause and reflect, and for many, including myself, we decided to take a leap of faith and leave our jobs. As I mentioned earlier, my situation was different as I was also dealing with a toxic workplace. In many respects, COVID-19 added more stress to my life. However, it created more opportunities to build resilience.

Police retention and recruitment is a major issue facing police departments across the country. National police organizations and researchers have found that low wages, poor benefits, and a lack of job security have caused this crisis. Why haven't we considered that it's the chief executive most responsible for this decline? Healthy cultures foster teamwork and therefore interest to work in that agency. To fix police retention and recruitment, police departments must address every issue and create an environment that encourages officers to stay in the profession.

If we want to bring back highly qualified and morally just police officer candidates, we need to evaluate our cultures. Each agency has its own identity, and too many agencies are duplicating what others are doing. Each community is different and made up of citizens who require specific needs for their town of residency. Police departments must embrace this and customize their policies and procedures based on what their community requires. Develop inside-out solutions, not the other way around.

For generations, police applicants showed up in droves and agencies got to select the best and brightest. That has changed, and so must we. It's time we meet applicants where they are. This may include holding community events where the chief executive meets with community members and answers questions about what it would be like working in the police department. The chief executive could also give a tour of the agency and use positive psychology to get potential recruits excited. Even if a chief has to knock door to door in their community to fill the ranks, then all options ought to be on the table. Sadly, too many executives are still waiting for candidates to come to them. Policing is a highly dynamic profession that is changing rapidly. If executives don't keep up with the ever-fluid environments, there is a huge community cost that comes with that ineptitude and malaise.

Us Against the World

The 1989 baseball hit *Major League* is a movie about a wealthy owner of a major league baseball team who wants the team to lose on purpose so she can relocate the team to a more enjoyable city. This owner, with nefarious intentions, puts together a team of misfits and over-the-hill players, expecting them to finish in last place. For half the season, the players on the team did not even know that their boss was working against them. With each passing game, the players started connecting and the team started winning. How could this happen when their own boss was working against them to lose? The general manager of the team finally approached the team manager and told him about the owner's plan. The manager got the team together and briefed the players on the owner's plan. As a team, they decided to "win the whole fucking thing" in spite of the owner. How many police officers are working now in agencies where their bosses are not actively working in their favor?

When teammates come together, magic happens. How can we bring teammates together? By creating strong cultures. *Major League* was a fictional story made by Hollywood, but it highlights an issue in organizational culture. The policing profession would benefit greatly from making a shift in how we select police executives. When we identify and select executive candidates first by their ability to bring people together, there will be a huge shift in organizational culture.

In 2022, the Philadelphia Phillies came into the season with lofty expectations. After a poor start to the season at 22–29, they fired their manager. They were twelve games out of first place and hadn't sniffed the playoffs in a decade. Beat reporters reported that the team was playing tight and not playing according to their talent levels. How can this be? The team was mostly healthy and there weren't major public spats. Why weren't they performing according to their capabilities?

Let's dive further. The Phillies promoted their bench coach to manager. Their new manager, Rob Thomson, is a baseball lifer and, by all accounts, a calm, steady man. Rob steadied the ship and the Phillies rebounded. The team came together and started playing according to their talent levels. The Phillies ended up going to the World Series and nearly pulled it off before losing to the talented Houston Astros four games to two.

What changed for the Phillies? I don't have inside information and did not talk to anyone from the organization about this book. My insights are from understanding how organizational culture, leadership, and mental health intertwine. I look for things that others don't. I watch nonverbal behavior. I have learned that our subconscious behaviors can communicate more than what we say. I observe teammate interaction and assess for camaraderie. I intently look for fraudulent or phony behaviors. I have been a part of tremendously successful units as well as unhealthy cultures. The more I watched the Phillies perform, interact and compete, something alarming hit me.

"These guys love each other," I told my son and wife. I started to notice how the players were not just teammates, they were turning into brothers. I have experience in this department.

When "brothers and sisters" start coming together, real collaboration takes place. The Me turns into We. There was a distinct moment watching the Phillies come back against the Braves in the Divisional Series, where I knew the team would go deep into the playoffs. It wasn't about winning and losing anymore; it was life and death. I could see the passion and focus in everything the players did and said. They wanted it bad, and that level of appropriate desperation and love for one another is what took them to the World Series.

As leaders, we must love our teams—*everyone* on our team. We can love every member of our police department, whether we like them personally or not. Love is the catalyst for successful and healthy organizations. Love is abundant, and our love for our families can also translate to those we interact with in the workplace. It's a different kind of love, but love nonetheless.

Love is how we rebuild cultures and bring the recruits back. Develop a mindset that your teams can rally around. Having an organizational identity goes a long way to filling in the gaps when times are darkest. Having a strong culture and identity is paramount to retaining talent.

Rebuilding Broken Cultures

Progressive police organizations are increasingly recognizing the importance of good leadership and organizational culture to achieve long-term success and stability. As such, many organizations are actively seeking to improve their culture and develop their leaders. This chapter will provide practical steps that organizations can take to improve their leadership and organizational culture.

1. **Analyze current leadership.** The first step in improving leadership and organizational culture is to analyze your current leadership. What are their strengths and weaknesses? What can be improved? How can their performance be measured? This can be done through a team analysis of the current leadership team or through the use of surveys,

interviews, and focus groups. This analysis will help to identify areas of potential improvement and provide a basis for making changes.

2. **Set vision and values.** Effective organizations have a clear vision and values, which are used to guide decisions and inspire collaboration among employees. Without a clear vision and values, organizations can quickly become stagnant and disorganized. Take the time to define the organization's goals and values, and provide regular communication to keep them front of mind.

3. **Develop a culture of trust.** An organization's culture is formed around the trust that exists between its leaders and employees. Without trust, employees will quickly become disengaged and unmotivated. Leaders should focus on building trusting relationships with their team by communicating openly and regularly, listening to concerns, and giving meaningful feedback.

4. **Promote transparency.** Transparency is an essential component of an effective organizational culture. Leaders should strive to create an environment in which information is freely shared and decisions are made in an open and collaborative manner.

5. **Recruit and retain talented employees.** An organization is only as good as its people, so it is essential to select and retain employees with the skills and attitudes necessary to contribute to a successful organization. Work to develop a recruitment process that attracts a diverse range of talented people, and ensure that you strive to retain key employees through competitive compensation and meaningful rewards.

6. **Encourage employee engagement.** Employee engagement is critical for an effective organizational culture. Leadership should actively engage their team by providing regular feedback and fostering a sense of ownership and team spirit.

7. **Foster collaboration.** Effective organizations recognize the benefits that come from the collaboration of their people. Encourage an environment in which teams feel comfortable working together and sharing ideas.

8. **Implement ongoing training and development.** Leadership and organizational culture can only improve when team members have access to ongoing training and development. Leaders should take time to identify areas of development for each employee and provide resources and opportunities to help them reach their potential.

9. **Improve compensation.** Police departments should also consider improving the benefits they offer to officers. This could include providing better health insurance, retirement plans, and other benefits that would make the job more attractive. In order to attract and retain officers, police departments should consider increasing salaries. This can be done by offering higher salaries to those who have more experience or by offering bonuses for completing additional training or certifications.

10. **Make policing fun again.** Serving fellow community members is fun! When performed optimally, policing can have positive effects on the community. Some of the best police officers and soldiers I know have a lot of fun on the job. When cultures promote fun and humor, it fosters added resilience and creates an environment where officers can be themselves.

Organizations can significantly improve their leadership and organizational culture through unique solutions. Strong leadership is fundamental to the success of any organization. Taking action to analyze current leadership, set vision and values, and promote engagement, collaboration, and development will lead to a more unified and effective organization.

By addressing these issues first, police departments can create an environment that is attractive to officers and encourages them to stay in the profession. This will ultimately lead to improved retention and recruitment of officers, which will help to ensure that police departments have the personnel they need to protect and serve their communities.

Retention

Retaining quality police officers is an essential goal for law enforcement organizations today. Without the people who commit to continuing to serve, the public safety mission of policing cannot be effectively carried out. There are a number of best practices that police executives can consider to improve the retention of police officers in their organization.

First, police leadership should prioritize creating a positive work environment for officers. This means providing adequate staffing, equipment, and timely feedback on performance and promotion opportunities. A positive workplace culture should be supported through a "quality of life" approach aimed at equipping officers and providing support for both personal and professional growth.

Second, compensation and benefits should be competitive with other law enforcement departments. Competitive pay packages give officers an incentive to stay with the organization. The pursuit of educational and training opportunities can also be used to attract and retain officers.

Third, effective leadership is essential for retaining quality officers. Leadership should strive to ensure that officers are supported in their work and that they feel valued for their contributions. This includes providing meaningful feedback and encouragement. Why would a high-performing officer stay in a stagnant agency? Departments should be setting the standard for the kind of cop they want. If they want unhealthy low-performing officers, hire executives who are not strong, collaborative leaders. Within a couple of years, top talent will leave as the standards fall. At my former agency, they are not assigning positions based on merit, and few of us can operate successfully in a system where the rules change by the week and standards are modified depending on the people involved. It stops becoming leadership.

Fourth, community engagement and partnerships can help create a positive image of law enforcement. Community engagement supports the agency's mission by fostering communication and trust between police officers and the public. Engaging with the community can also raise morale and demonstrate support from the public, which can strengthen relations between the organization and the officers. Human connection inside and outside the agency is essential.

Last—and I can't stress this enough—establishing strong mentorship programs will help ensure that newer officers have resources to help them adjust to their new role. Mentorship programs also demonstrate to officers that their efforts are appreciated and that their commitment to the organization is important. Cops will never know how much their leaders care until they're shown.

We can change and become better versions of ourselves. So can policing. Law enforcement organizations can create an environment that promotes successful police officer retention. Creating a positive work environment, offering competitive compensation and benefits, providing effective leadership, engaging with the community, and establishing mentorship programs are all key strategies to ensure officer retention.

Building a Supportive Workplace Culture

The mental and physical well-being of police officers is incredibly important both in terms of individual and workplace safety and efficiency. Police agencies must be proactive in offering initiatives to support the mental and physical health of their officers. This chapter examines the most practical and accessible ways that police agencies can improve wellness, focusing on those initiatives that could best benefit all those who work within the policing profession, particularly in times of stress and risk.

Creating a supportive work environment for officers is essential for fostering good mental health and well-being. A culture of open communication should be encouraged, and officers should feel supported and encouraged to talk openly about their concerns. Police agencies should provide educational opportunities on mental health topics, such as stress management, coping strategies, and self-care.

In addition, police agencies should make available access to mental health professionals and encourage officers to seek help when needed. If resources are available, there should be an opportunity for officers to access a confidential mental health counseling service.

Addressing Organizational Inequalities

We know now that organizational dysfunction has a direct correlation to officer wellness. The unhealthier the organization is, the less healthy the officers will be. Stress accumulates quickly and burnouts occur as the good officers are relied on even more. Police agencies should look closely at the underlying causes of job-related stress among officers. An important factor in addressing this stress is to ensure that officers are being treated fairly and without discrimination or bias. It is essential that police agencies create an inclusive work environment where officers can feel safe to express their concerns without fear of reprimand or judgment. Police officers are a competitive and judgmental population, none more so than against each other.

What made my situation challenging (and maybe you can relate) was the varying levels of treatment depending on who the officer was. The administration didn't treat everyone with the same lens, and it created confusion for me. I actually felt myself becoming more unsure of myself and began questioning if I was the problem. That's what happens when unwell people lead organizations: they take hostages by passing down their own unresolved trauma.

Organization Promoting Growth and Wellness

Police agencies must empower their officers to take proactive steps to take care of both their bodies and minds. In fact, if agencies led more in this area it would help to retain more experienced officers and also help distinguish an agency for recruitment. Police agencies can provide resources and access to physical fitness tools, which can help officers reduce the physical strain of their job. Moreover, police agencies should also emphasize the importance of a well-balanced diet, sleep, and relaxation. Officers should be *encouraged* to take **mental health days** to de-stress, relax, and pursue hobbies that bring joy and balance to their lives. By promoting a healthier and balanced workplace, we actually increase officer performance because we're considering their long-term health.

It is imperative that leadership encourage their officers to practice balance and implement boundaries in order to preserve their mental and emotional health. When leaders look out for the well-being of their teams, it helps to foster trust. A primary factor that leaders can do to help their officers is promoting a lifestyle where work is only a part of their officers' lives. Family time, downtime, and vacation should not only be provided but encouraged and promoted by leadership.

Effective police wellness initiatives integrate support, education, and prevention initiatives which can improve the mental and physical health of officers in the profession. Police agencies have a duty to ensure the safety and well-being of the officers they employ, and these initiatives are essential for providing the highest level of care and support. By adopting these suggested approaches and initiatives, police agencies can help to create an environment in which their officers can thrive. By being more connected to one another, police cultures can do their part to reduce officer suicide, which is the #1 killer of police officers. By connecting better, we are being proactive in keeping our high performers in place and feeling valued.

Recruitment

Recruiting police officers is an important task that many departments face due to new legislation, court rulings, or different strategies required. Finding the right candidates is not easy; successful recruitment efforts must ensure a fair approach to identifying candidates who have the interests and skills needed to be successful in their policing careers. For many agencies, they have civil service regulations to comply with.

In order to successfully recruit and hire talented candidates for police officer positions, departments have to prioritize certain steps for finding, recruiting, and hiring competent candidates. This section provides information and best practices on how to efficiently and effectively recruit police officers today.

Develop Targeted Recruiting Strategies

When recruiting police officers, it's important that department leaders develop targeted recruiting strategies. The type of candidate the department is looking for will determine what types of recruiting strategies are best. For example, if the department is looking for a large number of candidates with strong interpersonal and communication skills, then the recruitment process should emphasize those qualities in open houses, interviews, and advertisements.

If the department's vision is to create a bicycle unit in the next twenty-four months, recruit with that in mind. Recruit for soft skills because you can teach a young police officer almost anything and they'll soak it up like a sponge.

Be Flexible with Qualifications

During your search for high-quality police officers, departments should not be rigid about the qualifications that they require from candidates. Instead, departments should be flexible with what qualifications they require and take into account a wider range of applicants. This means that departments should consider applicants from diverse backgrounds, such as veterans, those with disabilities, and those with alternative career paths. There are countless police officer prospects each year who are passed over because of their "lived experiences," while it's those very experiences that will likely make them high-performing police officers. Maybe beyond some of the warts are polished rocks ready to be displayed. It takes an engaged and empathetic leader to spot these details. By being flexible with the qualifications, departments can ensure that the best candidates are chosen to serve in the police force.

Prioritize Quality Over Quantity

If you have five openings, don't focus on hiring five cops. Focus on hiring the "right cops," even if one or two end up making it. We got into bad habits of trying to fill the ranks in any way we could. I think that's a dangerous proposition long term. Departments should prioritize quality over quantity. Rather than relying solely on numerical numbers, departments should focus on finding candidates who have the skills, qualifications, and experience needed to serve their communities. Soft skills contribute to higher levels of performance over a longer period of time. Agencies should focus on emotional intelligence over rifle qualifications. This process must include conducting background checks, interviewing potential candidates, and evaluating their interpersonal and communication skills.

Ensure Transparency

When recruiting police officers, departments should ensure that the process is open and transparent. This means that the department should collect information and feedback from the public at every stage of the recruitment process. This should include holding public meetings to discuss the recruitment process, as well as keeping everyone informed about any changes in the recruitment plans. By being transparent throughout the recruitment process, departments can ensure that all potential candidates have the same opportunity to compete for a position in the police force.

Encourage Inclusivity

Unless you're an identical twin, no two humans are the same. So why don't we celebrate the uniqueness in others more? For cops, we don't like things we don't understand. Whether it's our lack of perspective, limited life experience, or low confidence in our abilities, when cops can't succinctly explain something or connect with it, it's either "lame," "dumb," or "weird." The more accepting we are of our differences, the better we'll do at recruiting the type of officer communities want.

When recruiting police officers, departments should strive to create an environment of inclusivity. This means that departments should welcome candidates from all walks of life who have an interest in serving their community. Policies should be established to ensure that all potential candidates are considered equally regardless of their race, gender, sexual orientation, or background. By fostering an inclusive environment, the department can ensure that the best and most qualified candidates are chosen to serve the community.

Call to Action

As the chief executive, what are you doing to improve your culture? Do you have a coaching/mentoring program to help your officers grow? If not, what's preventing you from doing so?

By making excuses for why we "can't" do hard things, we demonstrate to our officers that we are afraid to take risks and too stagnant to be bold. We set a culture of low expectations. Do you want your officers to have a "can do" attitude? I challenge you to lead more positively. Set the example that you want to see from your community and officers.

ACT IV

SUMMER

CHAPTER XII

RECOVERY

"IF WE DID ALL THE THINGS THAT WE ARE CAPABLE OF WE WOULD LITERALLY ASTOUND OURSELVES."
-THOMAS EDISON

Freedom

"Freedom isn't free." It's more than a slogan. I have that phrase tattooed on my forearm. More than ever, we see examples of how freedom in America is being challenged. Values that were once mandatory are negotiable in America today. I love progress and encourage it, yet with each passing year I feel less connected to my childhood and, in a greater sense, my personal identity—and not in measurement of time, but with the unrecognizable tapestry of how society is today compared to only twenty years ago. The acceleration of progress seems steep, though, as A.I. is now part of the lives of many professionals. In a society preaching diversity and inclusion, we are seemingly more divided by race, class, and gender than twenty years ago. Do you know what does not discriminate? Mental health challenges, including substance use.

The Power of Vulnerability

Sharing is caring. When we share our struggles, we remind others that they're not alone. Sharing our pain with each other can help us heal, too. Our society has found ways to rejoice in the downfalls of others. We label and stigmatize. Society provides a framework for things that are messy because we need to have explanations for everything. When we don't understand something, we build a box to fit around that of which we can't comprehend. Instead of listening and learning, we define. In my experience, sometimes we need to work backward to understand human behavior.

I'm diagnosed with post-traumatic stress disorder (PTSD), substance use disorder (SUD), and generalized anxiety disorder

(GAD). This is the only time I will reference my own diagnoses. I do not define myself by these diagnoses, and I will not allow others to define me according to medical issues. I no longer carry shame, and I made a courageous decision to use my lived experiences, both good and bad, as methods to connect with you and inspire you to heal and find joy.

As you hopefully learned throughout this book, there's much more to me than a bunch of letters after my last name. I am not my diagnoses or my educational experience. Neither are you. We are human beings, rich with life experiences of all shapes and sizes. It's the same reason I don't list my master's degree (MA), licensed private investigator (LPI), and certified recovery specialist (CRS). I'm very proud of them but they only tell a snapshot of my life. Just like I don't want to be judged on my poor behaviors, I also don't want you to judge me on my achievements. Don't we want to be judged on the content of our character, as Dr. Martin Luther King suggested? Have you been improperly defined by your diagnoses? What have you done to overcome?

Being vulnerable means suffering in public. It requires we share our struggles outwardly so others can heal inwardly. Moreover, sharing our pain leads to tremendous human connection. Connection and strong relationships are key to maintaining healthy workplace cultures. A core component of vulnerability is honesty, and when we develop cultures with trust and openness, it helps our teammates weather the impending storm. The personal lives of our teammates are not talked about enough through the lens of leadership and organizational culture. Our lives are one; there's no such thing as professional life and personal life. We live one life.

If I got into an argument with Kristen before work, I certainly carried that with me at work. When I finished my thesis for my graduate work, I was on cloud nine for a month, relieved and proud of the work I had completed. I guarantee I was a better cop for that month because I was a happier person. If our teammates are battling issues within their personal life, such as substance use or infidelity, they're more likely to recover if they're serving in inclusive cultures.

In 2010, after only two years on the job, I had a colleague open up to me about their mental health. I barely knew this officer, and they told me they wanted to hurt themselves. They were feeling much shame. I was 29 years old and was caught off guard by the impromptu conversation. I advised this officer I didn't know what to do and would find ways to help him. I immediately called my father and we got this officer into therapy within a week. That officer attended therapy for a while and rebounded. He's still on the job today.

Our organizational cultures become inclusive when leaders at the top foster trust. Trust can be formed by maintaining trusted information or secrets, sharing personal information that could be sensitive, not having siloed units or separate calendars, and executives sharing their own wellness journey. In Maine, Chief of Police Elliott Moya walked into his agency's squad room and shared with his officers that he was undergoing behavioral cognitive therapy, and the results have been promising. By the chief executive being vulnerable in his personal life, it helped break down any stigmas regarding mental health.

Many first responders and veterans do not come forward for help for fear of retribution from their chain of command. If executives can find a way to talk more about their personal journey of living a fulfilled life, it removes one major hurdle standing in the way of thousands of first responders and veterans.

Chief Moya is leading in a unique and innovative way in Maine. He formed a regional Officer Wellness and Resilience Conference that is different than other conferences I've attended on officer wellness. Chief Moya welcomes real talk and heartfelt solutions to help officers survive and thrive. Chief Moya had his detractors. That's what happens when change is being pursued. What I admire about Chief Moya the most is his courage and resolve. He is a bright and self-aware man. He understands that his pursuit of officer wellness will have obstacles and maybe even peers not understanding his mission.

Chief Moya is humble and carries himself in an unassuming manner. His outwardly quiet demeanor is at odds with the fire that rages inside of him. He desperately cares about the health and welfare of police officers. I recently went to write the names of police chiefs in America that most cops know based on their strong influence and reputation. I had zero names on the list and then it hit me: policing has no industry thought leaders. No one is leading the helm, modeling good behavior, collaborating with other leaders, and setting the standard for the profession. There are literally no policing thought leaders in America. In that case, it's rather easy to consider Chief Elliott Moya a thought leader as he is on the front lines of this officer wellness movement that is not going away.

What do you think prevents many police leaders from being courageous? For me, fear of judgment was a major disruptor. Even at moments when I wanted to be vulnerable, I ran through all the scenarios in my head. Could this cost me my job? Could this get me in trouble? Could this hurt me? The sad thing is in every moment I contemplated being vulnerable, it was because I needed support for something; yet I talked myself out of it due to fear. How many times in our organizations have we missed tremendous opportunities to help our teammates through something and we never even knew of their battle?

Substances

According to research—and it's consistent across the board—between 20–30% of active-duty police officers are using substances to self-medicate. I believe those numbers are higher. For one, I was the most accomplished member of my agency, and I was using drugs and alcohol to self-medicate my pain and trauma. I routinely watched my brothers and sisters engaged in binge drinking, talking about getting drunk, and have many first-hand stories of how cops got into trouble on the job and off due to alcohol. Officers, including executives, are using substances in shame, including prescription pills, to survive the profession. Add a toxic agency on top of the trauma that officers experience and it's a recipe for dysfunction.

The hard-hitting truth that will be hard for cops and leaders to hear is you will never become your best version while using substances to cope. I did it, and I was unhealthy. Today, I'm in recovery and don't drink alcohol. I lost thirty pounds in two years since retiring from the police, and I have more energy today than ever before. I have seen the worst side of cops; alcohol usually plays a role.

Many agencies don't have a wellness plan or promote one. Without positive influence from senior leaders, police officers will fall to the mean. Many are drinking and drugging as unhealthy ways to manage their stress. Stress management is an individual journey, in my opinion, but organizations also have a strong influence on their officers. If organizations are unhealthy, it will add more stress to the officer. If agencies are healthy, it will take off some of the stress for the officers. That means the chief executive's duties and how they execute them will either add stress to their officers or help them relieve it. Which chief do you want to be?

What is Recovery?

Recovery is the process of gaining back physical, mental, or psychological health, strength, and well-being. While most people think of recovery in the drug and alcohol treatment space, recovery can be applied more broadly. Recovery applies to mental health in that it focuses on helping individuals develop the skills and strategies necessary to manage their mental health and live meaningful lives and enjoy emotional well-being. Recovery focuses on reducing distress, increasing hope, and developing resilience and self-management skills. A key focus of recovery is to strive for optimal functioning rather than striving for symptom or diagnosis-free states. Reducing harm to ourselves by making healthier choices is not just recommended, it's required for a successful policing career.

Recovery is about finding a way to come back from difficult situations with a renewed sense of strength and purpose. For far too long, police agencies have been uncomfortable with imperfection. We prefer to work with cops who don't carry baggage or have scars. The fundamental problem with this concept is that it's just not realistic. Cops are humans and, therefore, at risk of the same life stressors that everyone else has. To make the situation bleaker, police officers continue to witness trauma at an alarming rate. Cops are changing emotionally and taking their lives at a concerning rate. As stakeholders continue to provide unsustainable and illogical solutions, many of the answers we need are right inside our agencies. We must do a better job of using our active recovery resources to maintain our health and develop higher levels of resilience.

As a person in recovery, I use all the tools on my belt to handle adversity. Pride and ego are not tools—they're inhibitors. They prevent us from reaching our potential and cause catastrophic effects on police culture. One of the main factors I deploy on my journey is *recovery capital.*

Recovery Capital

Recovery capital is the resources an individual needs to sustain recovery from addiction. Recovery capital includes factors such as a stable support system, reliable sources of income, a recovery plan, access to health care, and a positive attitude. Recovery capital can be thought of as the "fuel" that helps to motivate an individual's long-term recovery journey. The more recovery capital an individual has, the better the chances of sustained recovery. As I entered my recovery journey, I used my wife and kids as recovery capital. I hung their pictures up and would not allow myself to forget what I was fighting for. What in your life is significant enough for you to fight for? What in your life can you lean on that inspires you to reach your goals?

Maybe you're reading this thinking you can't stop drinking alcohol. Maybe you don't have a problem. Maybe you do and don't realize it. I'm the last one to tell anyone what to put in their body, but I challenge you to think about your own journey. Think about all the good you've done. Now think about the bad. We've all done good and bad things. The difference is what we choose to do after a bad thing. Do we sulk? Hide? Be bitter? Imagine if we could find ways to apologize. I think about that every day—how I can stop being bitter and start being better. I learned the more good I do for others, the less hurt I feel. I learned the more smiles I see from people, the less sad I get. I learned that by living a life of significance, the bad things I've done don't seem that bad. In the end, I'm focused on harm reduction as opposed to living a life of perfection.

Lived Experiences

Lived experiences refer to the individual personal experience of certain events or circumstances in one's life. It can be used as evidence-based research that can be used to inform and shape policy decisions, public speakers, as storytelling for advocacy or education, or various other purposes. This form of evidence—or testimony, as I like to call it—is based on real-life stories of different individuals and can be used for positive outcomes in terms of highlighting need gaps, bringing stories to life, advocating for change in the public and political space, and informing public opinion. Furthermore, it can be used to provide valuable insights into the real-world implications of decisions, provide context and support for policy initiatives, and demonstrate potential outcomes of proposals. It also provides the opportunity to create more meaningful, inclusive conversations and to explore a greater range of perspectives on a shared issue.

Our country has a checkered past in marginalizing people who look, act, and speak differently than "normal" people. There are many of us who experienced negative events and found ways to thrive. Maybe their ugly event was a criminal act or civil violation. They're embarrassing, I get it. But what if someone found a way to overcome? Don't we want to hear from them and learn what they did? Would we consider looking past someone's wrongdoing if they repented and corrected their behavior? Isn't that what it means to be human?

Here's what I can tell you with absolute certainty. In my life, I have met countless people who have failed and succeeded. They fell down and picked themselves up. There seems to be an asterisk next to their name in professional circles. Many of them are good enough for consulting positions, and I challenge organizations to consider hiring and promoting people with "lived experiences." These are individuals who haven't read about challenges; they lived them. They lead with resilience and hope. They're not perfect, but guess what...not a single person reading this will be. Let's challenge our perspectives, embrace our fears, and open our minds. There are some police departments who understand this, and they're not looking for the perfect candidate; they're looking for the *right* candidate for their culture. This approach could greatly benefit a declining profession.

Harm Reduction

Harm reduction is a term used in the context of recovery and is focused on minimizing the negative consequences of an addiction or other substance use behaviors. It's based on the principle of reducing the damage caused by drug and alcohol use and other risky behaviors, as opposed to attempting to stop them. This approach acknowledges that complete abstinence is unlikely for many people. With harm reduction, the overall goal is to reduce the harmful effects of an addiction or other substance abuse behavior. It involves identifying and managing risks while helping individuals still struggling with substance use to remain safe.

For cops, so many use alcohol and drugs as a coping strategy. They understand their actions and can develop a lot of shame as their use intensifies. Instead of not talking about alcohol use at all or pretending there are no alcohol issues inside their department, chiefs could be making the problem worse. Chiefs have a moral responsibility to the welfare of their officers, on duty and off.

A solution could be for agencies to acknowledge any alcohol and drug problems inside their agency and work through them. If you have good officers whose performance is suffering and whose personal life is deteriorating, I believe chiefs have a moral obligation to help their officers through the challenge. After all, it could be the result of something they experienced on the job. Not to mention the financial savings of retaining an officer and the utter joy of helping a good cop overcome.

There's organizational pride there and something to be proud of! We place cops in patrol cars and have them witness trauma on holidays and weekends. The least we could do for them is not ignore the signs of their demise, and if chiefs aren't going to be decent leaders and intervene, at least be good human beings by not kicking them on their way down. Sadly, sometimes that's too much to even ask.

We live in a world where perfectionism is the only mode in which we engage with others. We rarely share the negative parts of our lives, and by doing this, we have learned to suppress emotions. In law enforcement, the margin for error is even thinner, like a razor. No cop wants to be known as someone routinely out with an injury, and we don't want cracks in our armor. Our cultures are so unhealthy that we ignore harmful behavior that looks cool but judge harmful behavior that is nerdy. Alcohol problem? It's OK because the chief also has a problem. Drinking alcohol is cool.

What if you're a person who masturbates to manage stress instead of drinking alcohol? I hope I didn't offend you because that's a thing. The only issue with that is that it's not cool. Not only is it not cool, it's perverse, right? Only a sick son of a bitch would masturbate in his car. He should be fired. For the record, this is a real case of an officer who I read about in the news about five years ago before I started my journey toward knowing. A good-looking city police officer who was also a former Marine and had a beautiful wife at home was fired for masturbating in a retail chain parking lot after a shift one day. He was caught and reported. I read later that he was fired. I can only imagine the pain he was in. It's too easy to label him a deviant. I rejected that lazy labeling. Why did he do that? What was happening inside of him then? What did the masturbation do for him in that moment? I'm not a therapist, just a curious and caring person. I pray that the officer is OK wherever he is. I pray he is healed. I pray he's peaceful.

What if that officer is a good officer who reacts to stress in unhealthy ways? Are we really going to cast them aside and abandon them? Can't we support them just like the department drunk? Our culture must improve. We must extend our arms more freely and hug one another. We are not each other's enemy. We wear the same uniform and fight for the same cause. Let's support our fellow first responders through *all* their pain and baggage and provide trusting environments for them to heal in. If agencies promoted recovery and harm reduction, that could reduce the stress and shame officers carry from their substance use. They would also feel better supported where they work and more likely to remain with the organization.

At the heart of recovery and harm reduction is *respect* for people who are struggling with addiction rather than a judgment of their behavior. This approach looks at individual circumstances and develops targeted strategies that will help reduce the risks associated with hazardous lifestyles while finding ways to improve the overall quality of life. When recovery is promoted in police departments, there is a tremendous connection to the community that can occur through finding similar people with lived experiences. A police department can create better community culture by being more transparent and helping the community see that the men and women who patrol their streets are also their neighbors in AA meetings. This is a benefit of promoting recovery and focusing on harm reduction.

For cops, respect is a core element of feeling valued and appreciated. If the goal is to take better care of our people and keep the experienced cops performing at a high level, we must be more involved in our officers' lives. We achieve this by respecting our senior officers more and being more curious about how our personnel are doing. All of this must be done authentically and consistently, for anything else will not be taken seriously by the rank and file. Cops are street-smart and they cannot be fooled with half-truths and lazy efforts.

Imagine this scenario for a second... A good officer falls down and has to pick herself up. That officer is supported through her struggle and comes back better than ever. Wow, that's inspiring! That officer doesn't have to carry much shame around. The chief doesn't have to carry much shame around for abandoning an officer. The community keeps one of the good ones. Seems like everyone wins.

Solutions

As police departments work to develop a resilient and cohesive culture, incorporating recovery principles into departments' operational strategies is essential.

Here are some of the best ways police departments can use recovery to build a strong culture:

1. **Address trauma and stress.** Police work can be stressful and traumatic. When leads fail to acknowledge the stressors of the job and, more importantly, the change in their officer's behaviors, they knowingly or not are worsening the emotional and mental toll on the officer. Acknowledging the toll this takes on police officers is essential to restoring their physical, emotional, and psychological well-being and goes a long way to validating the changes going on inside the officer. Police departments can create trauma-informed practices to give officers the support and resources they need to cope and to promote resilience in the face of adversity.

2. **Utilize peer support programs.** Peer support programs can be invaluable for helping officers to cope with difficult situations such as substance abuse or PTSD. Peers are often better suited to provide the necessary support and understanding that officers may not find within their agency's chain of command. In my experience, both as a peer support officer and someone who went through a season of darkness, peer support has tremendous benefits in officer recovery.

3. **Promote self-care.** It's important for officers to take the time to care for themselves. Encouraging officers to prioritize self-care practices such as mindfulness and meditation is key to helping officers manage stress and stay in a healthy frame of mind. Mental health days should not be discouraged or stigmatized. Leads should build in scheduled downtime separate from their compensation package to sustain their career. The goal for any leader is to develop

and enrich each member of their agency. If executives want their officers to remain active and effective, self-care is mandatory. Without self-care, officers are susceptible to a host of problems.

4. **Lead with vulnerability.** Officers should feel comfortable talking with their leaders about their work-related stress and issues. Open dialogue from leaders regarding their own mental and emotional journey has powerful effects on our teams. When leaders are vulnerable, it promotes a culture where overcoming challenges is celebrated. Vulnerability leads to dialogue, which can help to create an environment in which officers can feel safe and supported. Officers already know the weaknesses of their leaders. By sharing and communicating with them, the leader helps to foster a culture of ownership.

5. **Strengthen teamwork.** Police departments should encourage camaraderie and collaboration between officers and staff. Working together can create an atmosphere in which officers are better equipped to handle adversity and rebuild after a traumatic event. Police departments could benefit from adopting a mindset of "let's get it right, regardless of who's right." When relationships are strong, healthy cultures allow for personal issues to be discussed as well. This should be the ambitious goal of police agencies: create cultures where officers can freely share their personal challenges in a collaborative effort to overcome them. This takes a consistent and authentic approach.

By incorporating these principles into their operations, police departments can create cultures that are strong and resilient. By cultivating an environment of mutual trust and respect, departments can also foster a sense of safety and well-being within their ranks. Wellness doesn't have to mean soft. Wellness doesn't have to imply weak. In fact, wellness signifies strength.

There is calmness when we lead with confidence. We tend to listen more and talk less. Our agencies can be a lot healthier than they currently are. These come down to decisions. If we shift our mindset to where our officers are our most critical asset, we'll invest the dollars into them because we prioritized them. Lately, with all the information available, I wonder how important officer wellness is to some leaders. Do they truly believe their officers are their most important asset when they don't prepare their minds for the inevitable? That's a cultural decision that must start at the top.

I hope you learned something new in this chapter. May it help you in your journey. If there's one highlight I'd like to focus your attention on to finish the chapter, it's this: **We can never become our best versions and perform at our maximum capabilities when we're using substances.** I'm not saying don't drink alcohol anymore; I just want to remind you that we're less healthy when we're using substances than not. For someone like me who stopped drinking alcohol, I'm repurposing all that energy and health into passion projects that can enrich others and the world around me. Maybe you're a social drinker, or you have a problem with dependency.

Wherever you're at in your journey, I wish you well and remind you that you can absolutely come back and show yourself grace and compassion. You're a good person! We all fall down. Welcome to the club. Now, it's time to get the hell up. I found a way up, and I know you can, too.

CHAPTER XIII

DREAM CHASING

"TODAY IS ONLY DAY IN ALL THE DAYS THAT WILL EVER BE. BUT WHAT WILL HAPPEN IN ALL THE OTHER DAYS THAT EVER COME CAN DEPEND ON WHAT YOU DO TODAY."
~ ERNEST HEMINGWAY

Dream-Chasing

In our capitalist system, most of us define success based on how much money we've earned and have. Wealthy people may believe they're good people because, for most of us, we've been conditioned to believe that money equals success. Poor people have told themselves that they're failures. I challenge you to reflect further than what society wants. Imagine the wealthy person reading this book who's been divorced multiple times and is in their sixties wondering why they're not happy. They've reached their professional destination with lots of money. Shouldn't they be more joyful?

We have encouraged our children to choose professions with high earnings. We've pushed them to chase high-status careers or ones that will bring us rewards. Here's what I challenge you to do: change the way you define success. For me, success was never about the bottom line. It's about feeling worthy of the love of those close to us and giving to the world more than I took. Being the best father and husband I can be is what success looks like to me.

Whichever way you define success, commit yourself to the process of becoming valuable toward a mission that serves others. Earning money in a way that is collaborative and serves humanity helps us to feel joy and pride. Focusing on earnings causes us to do things we never thought we would, and we end up carrying a lot of shame, which will not help us become joyful. If you want to chase money, just remember that not everyone equates earnings as a benchmark for success. Respecting everyone's personal values is critical for police executives as they create a plan for organizational success.

The World Needs Who You Were Born to Be

Actor. Singer. Professional athlete. Like every little kid who was born on the sunny side of rainbows, I have dreamt of big things for as long as I can remember. Every break was a sign. Every sign was a break. I can dream about just anything.

Taco restaurant owner. Coffee shop barista. High school football coach. President of the United States. Professional speaker. I don't just dream; I imagine the possibilities. I used to be ashamed of it, thinking how narcissistic it sounds. That's the last thing I want to be. The older and more experience I attained, I realized that we're limiting ourselves by not dreaming. Frankly, we're not giving the world what it needs. Instead, we're fighting against how God created us to fit in with everyone. How is that good for us, our families, or the community?

Today, I imagine how I can use my virtue for good in the world. I love people and want to be positive. I won't allow others to penetrate my force field anymore. Many will try, and I look forward to showing the world how love will defeat evil. I create a vision in my head where I'm fixing problems and using collaboration as a tool to provide solutions to the world. Here's what I learned about dreams: the only people who can deny them are ourselves!

I didn't grow up with money or famous connections. I "volunteered" for the military because I barely passed high school. In eight years of military service, I made less than most middle-class professionals make in a year. I went to war at 24 and was nearly killed. I returned home to my parents' bedroom and slept in the same bed I did as a boy.

Today, I have a wife, who's my best friend, three loving kids, a pain in the ass but lovable dog, friends and neighbors who love me, I earned a master's degree while depressed during COVID, own two small businesses, am a certified recovery specialist, was a detective, run two podcasts, do motivational speaking, write books, author a monthly newsletter, coach professionals in life and their careers, and coach both my sons' football teams. I still have time to watch my favorite team, the Philadelphia Phillies, every night and spend quality time with my wife. It took me 42 years to get to a place where I feel like I can make it to the end of today feeling joyful and purposeful with my family. Tomorrow is unknown and not promised. Forty-two years of scratching and clawing. Few things were easy for me, and everything was earned. Everything you will read in this book was the result of a lot of grit that I developed from a lifetime of failure and hard lessons.

I'm 5'7" and 180 pounds. I'm unremarkable or indistinguishable. I have no immediate identifiable and practical talents or skills. What God gave me was great, though. He blessed me with a freaking huge heart. It's this big heart that has gotten me into trouble and also brought life-changing experiences that wouldn't have happened without it.

God gave me self-awareness, which I believe is the most important trait to do hard things, forge strong relationships, and make the difficult change that many of us need to make at some point in our lives. God also gave me a solid work ethic. But it's nothing special; I have lazy streaks in me. What He gave me was a strong sense of duty and passion. I'm passionate in everything I do. When a passion project presents itself that also fulfills my sense of duty, my work ethic kicks into hyperdrive. I'm also a pesky little bugger. I don't give up when passion is swirling inside of me. I'm especially stubborn when people are falling around me. But again, nothing extraordinary. I imagine we're all much more similar than we are different. What attributes do you have that make you feel valued?

Every leg of the journey for me has been challenging, and I've wanted to quit a thousand times. I've sulked in the corner and thrown myself some amazing pity parties. There was a period where I couldn't pay my mortgage and I robbed Peter to pay Paul. I cried myself to sleep many nights, having nothing more than my faith in God and myself to prop me up. Even my wife Kristen had her doubts, and I don't blame her. There were some dark days. Days I struggled to get out of bed or off the couch. Days I hid in hotel rooms for fear of what's outside. Days I did sneaky self-sabotaging behavior to medicate myself through a toxic workplace. There were many late nights and worries for the future. But I'm here and much wiser and more resilient as a result.

Perfectionism will kill you, so stop trying to look and be great all the time. Social media and our capitalist cultures have misled us. If you want to be joyful, start chasing passionate missions that make you feel good. You may not be wealthy, but I guarantee you you'll definitely smile more. If money motivates you, find a career that brings you purpose first. Grind and grow. The money will come if that's what you want, but never commit yourself to earning money. That road generally leads you to wanting more and more. Like a dog chasing its tail, you may eventually get that tail, but you'll be dizzy and disoriented from the journey if you don't deploy values along the way.

The ongoing act of living a joyful life requires much work. We do not experience joy by happenstance. You will read how the slow burn of serving twenty-one years of military and police service started to decay my positive heart. Maybe you can relate and find answers here—that's my goal. Life is always throwing haymakers at us, and no matter how many we avoid, the Champ (life) routinely sneaks in devastating body blows that take our breath away. Sometimes they're so severe they cause permanent scars.

Here's what I learned as a master of falling down: we always have opportunities to rise! We can always come back or get up. Fighting with everything we have is a choice. Persistence and consistence. Do that and I guarantee you'll win, eventually. But we must be willing to display our scars for all to see. Vulnerability is required for higher levels of resilience. Suffering in silence only leads to despair or even death. We'll never reach our potential by keeping secrets. Too many secrets leave permanent scars on our hearts.

Haters Have Earned Our Empathy

I was the kid who wanted everyone to like him. Throughout high school I deployed humor and became a goofy kid trying to fit in. I always knew how to tell good stories and use my body and theatrics as one to hit home a point. There was a point where I was that guy saying, "Yeah, let me tell you about a time when..."

in an attempt to fit in and be accepted. Haven't we all done that? Deep down, we're all trying to be loved and accepted. That's a core human need, and I learned that often, when someone does something unkind to me, it's likely they are suffering from something in their life. We never know the battles raging within others. Something is causing them pain, or an experience triggered their fears and anxiety to want them to cause harm.

If we want to change police cultures (and the world), then we must be curious and love everyone. Even those who would do us harm. The criminal justice system as a whole could grow from such an arbitrary mindset. Life is gray, and meeting people where they're at, regardless of their situation, has positive healing powers. There's enough space in our lives to display empathy for those who harm us and forgive them—while never forgetting their behaviors and the results of those actions.

You see, as an overly trusting person, I've now learned how to tune out the words people say and evaluate them based on their actions. It's amazing how that simple shift in thinking has helped illuminate people to me. I see people much better now. All the good, the bad, the trying, the jealousy, resentment, anger, lusting, copying, searching; I can really see into people when I simply analyze their behaviors and subsequent actions. I can relate to many emotions and have learned to be comfortable sitting in the middle of a hurricane of trauma.

I'm nothing special, although they say you've mastered something when you do it for 10,000 hours. I'll leave that to others to evaluate. Look, the point is anyone can do it. We just need to care more and spend more time thinking about others. It's really that simple. Why are you a cop (or fill in the blank)? If it's to serve people and make a difference, and you're doing that, then I highly recommend working on yourself because once you realize you're already living your dream, your whole life will change. I guarantee it!

Dream-chasing is never about being rich and famous. Dream-chasing is about living a life of significance. It's about looking in the mirror and being so damn proud of yourself for the kind of person you've become. Dream-chasing is about tucking your kids into bed every night and telling them, "No matter what happens in this life, I will always be there for you. I love you," and getting a sweet hug and smile back because they believe it and trust you.

I watched so many cops spend their time at work when they could have been home with their families. For many, it's simply a choice; they choose to be at work than be at home working on the hard things. Those people are often the ones hurling insults at us and projecting their pain onto healthy people because healthy people like to help others. I learned to have great empathy for all of those people, including Chief Pathe, who has certainly earned my empathy and forgiveness. Often, it's the challenges in life that bring out our worse behaviors, and all of us could help society better by demonstrating empathy to those who harm us. We don't have to forget, but we can move on. Police officers deal with some circumstances unique to service professions.

Thousands of police officers are on single incomes and need to work a lot of overtime to support their families. It's rooted in love and sacrifice; my partner was one of them. Nick Oropeza was my partner/leader for most of my police career. Nick has four kids, and I watched him do little else but serve the community and provide for his family for thirteen years. He did little for himself because he recognized when he wasn't at work, he had to be at home. He also realized that he had to miss some family events because they needed the income, and time-and-a-half pay is hard to pass up. I had a front-row seat watching Nick week in and week out walk the tightrope of justice and family. Nick rarely complained and routinely talked about his gratitude for the life he has. Looking back, it was an inspiring example that I didn't appreciate.

SMA (Smartest Man Alive)

Nick Oropeza is the big brother I never had and one street-smart son of a gun. He was my first-line supervisor at the police department when I started. Little did I know that we would follow each other to every unit during my thirteen years. He was coincidentally six years older than me, just like I was with my little brother.

In the beginning it was slightly contentious between us. Honestly, Nick challenged the heck out of me and exposed my insecurities. I pushed Nick in uncomfortable ways and was a disruptor upon my arrival. Nick and I were both go-getters and learned quickly that "iron sharpens iron." As tough as it was in the beginning, Nick and I have the same values and morals. Despite how different our personalities are, we found a way to make it work. Day by day, we leaned on our similarities. We can talk about our differences, and we should celebrate our uniqueness because when we're trying to perform at a high level, it requires synergy and collaboration. Everyone on the team has to buy in and make sacrifices. Nick and I not only came together but ended up becoming the best of friends. Nick's experiences as a father had a tremendous influence on me. His wisdom would be heavily needed as I struggled in silence through my thirties.

Throughout my thirties, I needed a strong man to challenge me and remind me of what's important. After Fernando, Nick is the most virtuous man I know. I'm so fortunate and melancholy to have watched him take beating after beating, fighting for what's right. Even when every other cop in the department complied with the unfair treatment of some of their brothers, Nick's sheer will allowed him to stand alone and take the heat. I've never seen him compromise his values, and there were times I suggested he do so to save himself from heartache. Nick resisted every time. I guess you could say Nick has rubbed off on me. I don't know where I'd be without Nick, but I do know I wouldn't be dream-chasing without him in my life.

Nick helped me to learn that dream-chasing for me is about always doing what is right and always speaking the truth for what is right. I have no doubt that God brought Nick into my life. Just like Fernando was an integral part of my early development, Nick was an integral part of my later development. We need good people around us to flourish. There was a period of many years where Nick made every right decision, and he earned the nickname SMA (Smartest Man Alive). SM-AH helped me tremendously, and he has his fingerprints all over my career and life.

Do you have a positive influence in your life right now that you take for granted? What's holding you back from meeting them in person and telling them how much you appreciate them?

Just the Two of Us

When I returned home from Iraq, I had just turned 25. I returned home from war a different man—a battled-tested man to everyone, but very much still a boy. I still didn't know who I was, yet I felt expectations to be a certain way. What was the path God intended for me? One thing is for sure: I was ready for stability.

I wanted a real relationship. To love and be loved. To protect just one person with my life instead of hundreds or even thousands who didn't know me. War provided perspective, yet I still lacked the wisdom needed to be a good provider. Wisdom comes from experience, so it was time to hit the dating scene.

There were many relationships throughout my Army career, and now that I was freshly discharged, I was in a new headspace. One aspect few combat soldiers discuss, and it continues to swirl within me, is the desire for inner peace. It's a lifelong mission that drives me quickly into passion projects. It also can manifest in unhealthy ways, such as pulling out of something with little warning. I'm like a streaky home-run hitter in baseball; I will go on such cold streaks of poor self-esteem and confidence. However, there are times when I'm the best hitter on the field. Like my favorite current pro player, Kyle Schwarber, I've learned to hit bombs and be OK with striking out 200 times in a season.

No matter what it is or how much I love the project, if I begin to feel fear, my brain goes into survival mode. I then look for places to hide and stay safe. It's an instinct and reaction I constantly work on improving. I've learned how to rewire my brain through discipline and focus. As a person always searching for inner peace, few things soothe an aching soul more than love.

I dated a few women over the first few months I was discharged and was definitely pressing too hard. I was aligning myself as the "knight in shining armor." I had yet to recognize in myself my own deficiencies as I tried to be the "hero" for everyone else. Those cracks would slowly break open over the next decade-plus.

When I want something, I'm tenacious. The dating scene wasn't working, and I decided to take the summer of 2006 off to focus on myself. Ever since I was a little kid, I wanted to be a pro baseball player. I played in high school and tried to play on adult teams in the Army. Life as an infantry leader was too demanding.

With no distractions, I decided to pursue my dreams. I know the chances of me playing on the Phillies was 0.00001%, yet God did not wire me to simply not try. Plus, I loved baseball more than anything. I dreamed on patrol and waited in line at the internet center to get online time to check Phillies scores from Iraq. I returned home with new experiences, namely IEDs blowing up our vehicles, being ambushed, witnessing violent interrogation scenes, etc. These trauma-based experiences created energy in me where I want to find something positive to take away the pain I'm feeling. There were things in this world I took for granted. So, at 25, I tried for the local community college team. My old high school buddy helped train me. I played a fall season with the club and realized quickly that dreams don't translate to reality. I finally put my baseball dreams to bed. I would have to help the Phillies in other ways.

Back to love…

An hour away in Bethlehem, Pennsylvania, another 25-year-old was in her townhome mourning a failed seven-year relationship. My wife, Kristen, born thirteen days before me, just experienced a devastating breakup after a long relationship. It was traumatic for her. Kristen and I were strangers to one another.

It's early 2006 and MySpace was all the rage. MySpace was the first social media platform I used that allowed me to "brand" the page. I customized it with country music and pictures of friends and family.

I was still living at my parents' home while figuring out my next moves, being a 25-year-old college freshman and training for my baseball dreams:) As a (semi) grown man, I was sleeping in my twin bed from childhood. I woke up one day with a message in my MySpace inbox:

> *Hi Chad, I saw that you were in the military and wanted to thank you for your service to our country. You must be very brave. Thank you.*
>
> *Kristen - Bethlehem, PA*

The message was so sweet and kind. The simplicity and brevity caught my eye.

The profile picture was of a woman who, beyond the immediately apparent physical beauty, had a smile that seemed so warm. I look into eyes and smile when I meet people. Her bio description said, *Elementary teacher, cheer coach.*

Ohhhhh…this is promising, I thought. *She's beautiful, patriotic, appears kind, and she's a teacher!* So I did what every rational man with half a brain does…

Barely anything.

I sent a simple reply and closed my laptop…

> *Thank you, Kristen. While we don't need praise, it's nice of you to say. Thanks again and have a great day.*

Fast forward three months, and I'm working as a private investigator in Seattle. It was summer and I was bored watching the house of a person with a disability. The insurance company believed something was amiss and paid to have this person's activities documented. It was a fun job to have in transition. I did not realize how being a P.I. would later become a career path. I sat in the back of my company minivan, killing time from boredom.

I opened my MySpace page. Social media was new then, and it wasn't something I spent a lot of time on. I read old messages, and right there at the end of my inbox was Kristen's message.

I remember being confused. I read the response I wrote her and refreshed myself on our conversation. Has there ever been a time when something should have been so obvious and you couldn't see the forest through the trees?

"Don't screw this up, big guy," the inner voice said.

> *Hello, Kristen,* I started typing. *This is Chad from MySpace. You messaged me a few months ago. I'll be in your area for a case next month and was wondering if you'd like to have dinner together?*

On July 22, 2006, I arrived in Bethlehem, Pennsylvania, from out of town. I remember being so excited. The butterflies, checking the mirror a thousand times, making sure I had gum, repeating her Portuguese last name over and over.

I walked into the restaurant, and standing there in the foyer was Kristen. She was wearing these cute jeans, open summer sandals, and an adorable shirt. She extended her hand straight out and gave me a firm handshake. She looked me in the eyes with a big smile and said, "Hi, I'm Kristen!" I remember it like yesterday. She took my breath away.

Kristen had me off my game all night. She was so sweet and funny. She was also wildly successful, comparatively speaking, and I remember feeling imposter syndrome a few times.

We're thirteen days apart and lived an hour away from each other. We were strangers that somehow collided together online when that was still frowned upon.

Kristen was already in her sixth year of teaching, and I didn't have a job.

She had a master's degree and I barely earned a high school diploma.

She had her own townhome that she bought herself. She even had a tiny and adorable dog in this house. I was sleeping in my childhood twin bed at my parents' house.

Kristen set an early example in my early transition of what the possibilities could be. What Kristen didn't know was that less than a year earlier, when I was in Iraq, I reenlisted for six years because I assumed I would just be a grunt for the rest of my life.

I had no belief in myself to do anything other than being a soldier. My leaders even told me, in the endearing ways grunts talk to each other, "What else are you going to do? This is who you are." Shame on me for believing them.

So, I raised my hand and took the oath. Six more years. It upset my father because he thought there was more to me than soldiering, as proud as he was.

The next day my lieutenant informed me that there was a paperwork mishap and we had to redo the oath and paperwork.

"No, thank you, sir," I quickly shot back. God blessed me with self-awareness. I knew something was wrong. Or maybe something was right :)

So instead of making the Army a career, I came home at 25. Kristen wasn't aware of this on our first date.

The nights in Iraq where we could have been killed and the mishap of losing my reenlistment paperwork were signs from God.

I learned to develop a healthy desperation that I believe I still carry with me today: life is short, and tomorrow isn't promised. When I know I want something, I go after it.

Three weeks after our first date, we had our third date. I intentionally did not kiss Kristen on the first two dates. I was going to do this right. Our first kiss was on a stump in the Pocono Mountains. It was a beautiful sunny August day. That was the day that changed my life forever. I told Kristen I was going to marry her and she gave me the bug-eyes emoji face.

She knew, though...

How could she not?

She must have felt how serious I was.

I put the work into being a good man. Every single day. I mess up often and it's because of Kristen's grace and love I pull myself back. Kristen has earned a man that respects her and God knows I made mistakes early in our marriage.

I was so confident that I was going to marry her. As a matter of fact, there have only been two times in my life when I was 100% certain about anything: when I decided to leave policing for entrepreneurship and when I wanted to marry Kristen.

Kristen is an angel sent to me from God. He provided this beautiful human to me when I needed her the most. I tell her this as much as I can, yet I must be better. Every day I look for ways to improve and be a better lover. Yet, I fail often. It's the winding journey of an interesting life that gets me up each day. We have three kids—Lucas, Malia, and Marcus—and although life is rarely easy and even less convenient, we have found a way to love and be loved. We have learned how to see each other and value each other for our uniqueness. We have found ways to collaborate and be selfless. We're on our way to mastering communication—how to understand things we don't agree with.

I challenge you today to think of the relationships in your life. What can you do to improve them?

My Dream for You

More than any single thing, I hope you desire to live a life of significance. When we have the courage to step into our true potential, we won't have to hurt others along the way. When we love fiercely, we're much more prepared to fight racism, nepotism, favoritism, hypocrisy, cronyism, and political patronage.

I wrote this book as a labor of love for the policing profession. She broke my heart with how toxic she is, yet I found a way to give back to her for all the good she did for me. I became a man on the job and grew up wearing a badge on my chest. If this book can help the policing profession become more empathetic and inclusive of all personalities and experiences, then I have done my job. Truthfully, I'd rather not have to write this book. I'd rather be serving human beings on the front lines like I have for so long. Alas, that's not the path God has for me. He's calling me somewhere different now, and for the first time in my life, I will not balk and pause. Full speed ahead.

As I write this, I think of the countless police officers struggling right now. I think of those who are continuously putting themselves in harm's way (mentally, physically, and emotionally) for their communities. I think about the cops (really anyone) who were betrayed by those they cared for. I think of the families who lost a loved one to suicide. I think of the kids who grew up in an abusive home because mommy or daddy couldn't work through their shit. I think of the leaders who are taking hostages and prisoners with their selfish pursuits. I think about the cops sitting in their patrol car right now, pondering what their life would be in a different profession. What really keeps me up at night is the thought of the 25-year-old rookie unprepared and afraid to perform to their capabilities because of the political landscape in this country. How is one expected to succeed and maintain their sanity?

Maybe you have to leave your agency for inner peace. Maybe you have to leave the profession. I'd like to propose a third option: **growing**. What if you stay? What if you put the work in to heal? Imagine a scenario where you're sitting in a therapist's chair, working out your baggage. What would your life look like as you repair relationships? Maybe the only change you need to make is yourself. Empowering! So, what are you waiting for? I can't help you anymore. It's all on you now. I know you can do it because we all have something inside of us that we often suppress because we don't want anyone to judge us for it. So we hide in the shadows. Have you ever considered that the one thing you're most hiding may be the calling that you were created for?

If you're reading this chapter as an executive, then I assume it has made an impact on you. I bet you've done some amazing things in your career, and you may have hurt someone along the way. That's life. The only challenge I issue to you is to stop making excuses. Fix it! Whatever it is. I promise that when you work on your personal baggage, you'll become a better leader. I even bet you'll become a better spouse, friend, and neighbor too. That's the power of vulnerability.

I wish you well on your journey. I know you can do the hard things in front of you! Find your self-confidence and chart a course toward servant leadership. If you stick with it consistently, there will be a time when someone on your team will make a passing comment at 3 p.m. on a random Tuesday: "Hey, thanks for everything. I enjoy being here." That's a healthy culture, and it's only attainable when we select the right person to lead our police agencies.

Through all the mud and blood, leaders roll up their sleeves in the act of servant leadership. If our teammates are enjoying themselves and making an impact, then we've done our job. If leaders are tired, battered, and bruised, chances are they did their job. When leaders consistently sacrifice for their teammates, the scars they develop become like rings on a tree stump. With each scar, leaders repurpose their experiences to help the next leader. As leaders, we must inspire men and women. We largely achieve this by showing our scars. When our teammates see our scars on display, there's an immediate buy-in. Scars could be physical, mental, or emotional. Some are easier to see than others. The skill of highly effective leaders is showing their teams just enough scars to develop trust and synergy, but they save scars for the next hard mission when their teammates will need further inspiration.

Goodbye & Call to Action

First, I want to thank you again for buying and reading this book. I hope you're sitting on your favorite chair or laying in bed feeling proud that you purchased this. I hope you have a fire burning in your belly to get to work. If this book impacted you, please share it with someone who could also benefit. Let's help as many people as we can.

Second, you may be a little overwhelmed after reading this. There are heavy themes and topics in this book. If you're like me, you may even be intimated with the work ahead of you. It's normal to feel whatever emotion you're feeling. If you're scared or anxious about anything in your life, remember that no emotion lasts forever. You are most likely trying your best in life and have problems to work through like the rest of us. Show yourself grace. You've earned it.

If you're currently in a leadership role, the primary advice I can give you is to never lie to your teams. Ever. A simple lie will ruin all momentum gained. A white lie isn't even acceptable. Many police organizations or private companies lie routinely to their teams, residents, or clients. We justify the lies in our heads when in reality, we're drifting further away from our personal and organizational values.

When organizations move the goalposts back, a white lie intended not to offend someone can turn into a criminal lie intending not to get caught. Every bad act comes with a cost. So does every virtuous one. What I've learned these past four years is there is little difference sometimes between virtue and corruption. Although they're polar opposites, it's often the small decisions of some that carry the biggest consequences.

Chase purpose. Be virtuous. Love unconditionally. Serve as an example. This is the way.

Like Ferris Buehler says in the 1986 cult classic *Ferris Bueller's Day Off*, "Life moves pretty fast. If you don't stop and look around once in a while, you could miss it." I'm working to make the most of my opportunities. I don't know where I'm heading, but I invested all my money in this venture. I even needed the assistance of strategic partners who ended up being "angel" investors, in the literal sense. We struggle to pay our bills like anyone else. In some way, it's like being a kid all over again but from the other side. If I had planned better for my exit from the police department, I might have had a better shake. I did the best I could with the cards I was dealt. That's all any of us can do. By sharing my story, I'm focused on serving you, which also helps me. We heal and recover better aloud and together.

What's your first order of business as soon as you close this book? Contacting a therapist? Calling an old friend you hurt? Apologizing for something unkind you did or said? Hugging your kids? Call a staff meeting? Wherever you go first, just know that I'm proud of you. Change is not easy, and showing up each day is half the battle. Believe in yourself. If you have nothing else in this world, believing in yourself is the only true factor to consider when dream-chasing. Find a way to believe in yourself because once you do that, you will be the leader you were born to be. Our dreams are different, but the ingredients needed to make them are the same.

Thank you for connecting with me over this book. Whether you feel it or not, there's synergy between me writing this book and you reading it. We connected over our collective experiences. If you want more connection, reach out to me and share your journey. We're in this fight together.

I love my family, the noble profession of policing, and this country. No one person or institution is perfect. Aim for excellence and be happy with the results. You will fail a lot, and that's what you want. There's success (winning) and learning (losing). Only one of them is enjoyable, and both are beneficial for us.

I will share some personal pictures and journal entries at the end of this book. The journal entries are very personal to me, but I'm sharing them for two reasons. First, to further show you my journey of recovery from mental and emotional health challenges, and second, to highlight the importance of human connection. My wife is a selfless and collaborative life partner. I want you to see how important it is to have a significant other who encourages and supports you. Strong connection is what a successful and healthy police officer needs to weather storms.

Don't waste the time you spent reading this book. Try being unique and incorporate some of these suggestions into your leadership routine. What's the worst that can happen? I will **promise** you this: Lead with **love,** and you'll *always* be an effective leader. I even came up with an acronym for you to remember because I know how much cops and soldiers love "easy-to-remember" acronyms:

F – Faith (in something)

R – Relationships

E – Experiences

E – Express gratitude

D – Do kind things for others

O – Optimism

M – Mindfulness

Incorporate FREEDOM into your daily life, and you will be on the path to leading with honor and living a life of significance.

Much love and peace,
Chad
chadbmotivates@gmail.com

APPENDIX

Adverse Childhood Experiences Survey (ACES)

Instructions: Below is a list of 10 categories of Adverse Childhood Experiences (ACEs). From the list below, please place a checkmark next to each ACE category that you experienced prior to your 18th birthday. Then, please add up the number of categories of ACEs you experienced and put the *total number* at the bottom.	
Did you feel that you didn't have enough to eat, had to wear dirty clothes, or had no one to protect or take care of you?	☐
Did you lose a parent through divorce, abandonment, death, or other reason?	☐
Did you live with anyone who was depressed, mentally ill, or attempted suicide?	☐
Did you live with anyone who had a problem with drinking or using drugs, including prescription drugs?	☐
Did your parents or adults in your home ever hit, punch, beat, or threaten to harm each other?	☐
Did you live with anyone who went to jail or prison?	☐
Did a parent or adult in your home ever swear at you, insult you, or put you down?	☐
Did a parent or adult in your home ever hit, beat, kick, or physically hurt you in any way?	☐
Did you feel that no one in your family loved you or thought you were special?	☐
Did you experience unwanted sexual contact (such as fondling or oral/anal/vaginal intercourse/penetration)?	☐
Your ACE score is the total number of checked responses	

Chad's Personal Journal

April 4, 2019

Tonight is the sergeant's promotional exam. I'm not nervous at all, just anxious for the next steps. My whole career has seemingly brought me here tonight. It's time to continue the pursuit of leadership. I'm not even sure I want this. I know what it will take to succeed, and it will be hard on my family. Lots of sacrifice is needed to lead properly. This must be a family decision. But I love the department and community. They need me to do this because that's what I've been preparing for. What was the point of committing myself as a student of leadership if I don't jump in with two feet? It's for the guys and the residents. Not about me. The promotion would mean I go back to patrol, which is rotating shifts, nights and weekends. It will require an adjustment. I don't want to go back to patrol but I also can't be selfish. This is a family and department decision. I hope I do well...and I pray I make the right decision.

Lately, really for the past 90 days, I have had some off days. Full-fledged panic attacks. Feelings of extremely low self-worth. It seems that a lot of it stems from always trying to serve and please others. It's an impossible task, especially when it's for people who purposely don't acknowledge the efforts. They use it against me. I see what goes on and sometimes I just let it happen because I don't want to rock the boat. I grit my teeth and punch my leg fighting against myself. There are plenty of times I speak up too, and that causes me anxiety, not knowing how it would be received. People don't like when you question them. I will always do what's right. I often sit at work and dream of doing something different. I don't enjoy this job nearly as much as I used to. I understand that it happens as you get older and do the same job for over 10 years. It's part of life. I just thought I would find something I love greatly forever. I see some cops who love this job in year 20 just as much as in year 1. I also see many who are miserable in year 20. I guess I'm wired differently. What changed?

September 27, 2019

I finally came to grips with something that I've been hiding. I've been using painkillers. I'm such a piece of shit. I'm not even sure why I'm doing it. I'm not a drug addict. It's odd because I don't use daily. I don't know why I do it, then not do it for several weeks. It feels so good to be on them and calm my brain down. Man, what a scumbag I've become. The worst thing is, I rationalized it and had no choice but to keep it secret because of my career and family. I feel ashamed. So much shame. Why am I doing this? It was never about a physical addiction—it's more of a mental addiction. I find ways to get them and save them all for one night and look forward to that night to use them. I melt away in the couch and forget about life for a few hours. Then I go to bed without a problem, wake up in the morning with the kids, and go about life. It might be 1–2 weeks, sometimes a month before I would do it again. I always know it's wrong and it's hard not to think of myself as a selfish person because I'm being selfish right now. God, am I really that way?

April 12, 2020 (Easter)

Wow. What a moment. I'm working night shift overnight into Easter morning. At 4 a.m., I drove past Lansdale Catholic High School and prayed at the crosses on the side lawn. I was feeling down. It comes and goes. Sometimes I feel so alone, so misunderstood that I cry. I saw those crosses on the side lawn early on Easter morning and was immediately inspired by Jesus's death and resurrection. I got out of my car and stood at the base of the crosses in what seemed like an eternity. In reality it may have been ten minutes. I was praying and asking God to tell me what I'm supposed to do. After all, Kristen tells me I need to ask Him more. Put my faith in Him. And I swear at that moment upon the crosses, I heard a voice say softly, "Lead Them." In a time where I'm desperately searching for a purpose, I'm constantly asking myself, "What is my destiny?" Then there was that voice from beyond the crosses, "Lead Them." I didn't know what it meant until I gathered my thoughts. It hit me as if a switch was turned on. Lead Them referred to my children. There is no task in this world more sacred than that of being a father. A leader to guide them and show them the way. To hold their hands and walk the path with them. For a father's love is boundless. I see the way my children look at me, like their hero. Their protector. The light in their lives. A beacon to guide them in the storm that will shine even on the darkest of nights. The mere thought of my family made me cry. And I cried and cried. I have so much to be grateful for. My beautiful family. My wife. My kids. The air I breathe. I look down at my wrist and see the names of men that no longer breathe. We're only left with their memories. My life still goes on. Jesus rose today to show us eternal life. But, also, Jesus will come back to judge the living, and I must continue to try as best I can to keep moving. I cried at the beauty and the pain. I'm parked here now in my patrol vehicle, looking at the crosses and listening to a track from "I Still Believe." The tears are still rolling down. It's so darn beautiful. There was a time in Iraq where I didn't think I was going to make it. I thought I would have no legacy. No family. Now I have an amazingly tender and loyal wife. Sweet and graceful. Men spend lifetimes looking for someone like her. She blessed me with three children, who I love more than anything. I would die for them without ever thinking about it first. It's instinctual. This moment will stay with me as a reminder for all the good that God has shown me and the vast responsibility every day to be the man my family needs. 0400 hours on 12 April 2020—a special day indeed.

April 12, 2020 (Easter night)

I'm back on duty, almost midnight. I shared my experience with Kristen. She opened my eyes. Here's our text exchange:

> **Kristen:** *Wow....good for you! If you put your faith in God, I told you he will show you the path you should take. He is in the driver seat and has a greater plan. Maybe right now that is the big picture, not always looking ahead to something better, but enjoying what you have right in front of you... being present in the moment.*

Chad: *I'm looking to "lead" cops that I never stopped to think that leading my own children was most important.*

Kristen: *Anyone can be a dad, but being a good father is a lot of work...it's not an easy job and it will be the greater/biggest job you'll ever have and it will always be the one you are most proud of. One day you will retire as a cop but you will never retire as a father...*

Chad: *U are right. And I know I'm a good dad. Present and loving. But maybe that's the highest I go. And if that's the final destination for me then I should feel honored. That was the point of last night. It made me realize that.*

Kristen: *And when you look back you'll say you were proud of your service in the military and law enforcement but that will never weigh more than your family / kids.*

Chad: *I don't think I ever thought of my family as an "accomplishment." But u are right. Last night changed my view, my state of mind.*

Kristen: *Well you should....it's a full time job and takes a lot of commitment & dedication.*

Kristen: *PS your strength is leading ... you are always leading no matter what your role is. You don't need a fancy title to be a leader.*

Chad: *Thanks Goomie. I really appreciate that. I guess that's my point. I was down on myself for not being able to get a "leadership role." BUT I HAVE ONE!*

Kristen: *That's my fave thing about you. If I had to pick only one reason why I love you....clearly there are many....that one reason would be that I feel safe with you. My heart feels protected. And when I need something I know I can turn to you.*

Chad: *I always want people to depend on me. I need to know that u do. I will never let u down.*

Kristen: *That's not an easy thing for people to say about others .... there's a lot that comes with that statement. Your love & loyalty are what I love best about you.*

Chad: *Wow. I can't respond. Thank U. I work hard for that trust and dependability. Thanks for loving me.*

Kristen: *Stay true to yourself and keep being you. Believe everyone that has had the pleasure to know you in some way would say that about you. That's what makes you special ...*

Chad: *This is the deepest and most sincere analysis you've ever provided me with.*

Kristen: *...You are passionate and loyal and people respect that.*

Chad: *Ur making me cry. Happy cry. We can end it there. Don't ruin it. Ha.*

Kristen: *Lol. Good night. I love you very much.*

Chad: *I love you to the moon and back.*

LEADERSHIP CONTRACT

I, _______________ _______________________, PROMISE and SWEAR to:
(rank) (name)

1) Always be truthful.

2) Place the needs of the community and the welfare of the team above my own.

3) Never ask a teammate to do anything illegal, unethical, immoral, unkind, or offensive.

4) Regulate my emotions properly and have a temperament that fosters trust and credibility.

5) Use this position to add value to the lives and careers of every teammate by mentoring, training, encouraging, supporting, and treating everyone fairly and equitably.

6) Give every willing resident opportunities to cultivate close bonds with the police department.

7) Share all knowledge, training, resources, mentorship, and experience with every teammate.

8) Retain an executive coach to hold me accountable as a team leader.

9) Always be open-minded and never cast judgment.

10) Promote an inclusive and accepting culture.

11) Always maintain confidentiality.

12) Lead a virtuous, honorable, faithful, and healthy lifestyle so that I can fulfill my primary duties of leadership.

13) Give maximum effort in every project, duty, assignment, relationship, encounter, and task.

14) Lead __________________ P.D. in a manner that will bring great pride and respect; collaboratively lead with others to make _________________________ the desired community in PA.

____________________________ ________________________________

Signature Date

____________________________ ________________________________

Accountability Witness signature Name

TEAMMATE CONTRACT

I, ________________________________, PROMISE and SWEAR to:

1) Be team-focused in all operations and functions (there are no individuals).

2) Place the needs of the community and teammates' needs above my own.

3) Be a "professional" in all aspects of my career and life.

4) Use my position as a police officer to cause positive effects on others.

5) Let a teammate know if I'm struggling with mental, emotional, or physical wellness.

6) Give every willing resident an opportunity to cultivate close bonds with the police department.

7) Always support a teammate.

8) Tell the truth.

9) Respect every living thing to the highest degree.

10) Be positive and solutions-oriented.

____________________________ ____________________________

Signature Date

____________________________ ____________________________

Accountability Witness signature Name

____

Date

Made in the USA
Middletown, DE
30 September 2023